ARCHDUKE FRANZ FEF
AND THE ERA OF ASSA

ALSO PUBLISHED BY ROYAL ARMOURIES

Arms and Armour of the First World War (2017)
Saving Lives: Sir Arthur Conan Doyle and the Campaign for Body Armour, 1914–18 (2017)
Stumbling Towards Victory: The Final Year of the Great War (2018)

ARCHDUKE FRANZ FERDINAND AND THE ERA OF ASSASSINATION

Lisa Traynor

ROYAL ARMOURIES
TALKING POINTS SERIES

Published by Royal Armouries Museum, Armouries Drive, Leeds LS10 1LT, United Kingdom

www.royalarmouries.org

ISBN 978 0 94809 288 6

Edited by Martyn Lawrence

Typesetting by Out Of House Publishing
Printed by W&G Baird

10   9   8   7   6   5   4   3   2   1

A CIP record for this book is available from the British Library

For Roy

CONTENTS

ILLUSTRATIONS

PLATES

Plates A–D are situated between pages 20 and 21, and plates E–J are situated between pages 52 and 53.

A   Top: Spanish Velo Dog revolver in 5.5 mm (XII.6996). Bottom: Spanish Velo Dog revolver in 6.35 mm (XII.4839). Both examples date from the early 20th century. © Royal Armouries.
B   A presentation Browning Model 1900, with inlaid gold (PR.8689). © Royal Armouries.
C   The Browning Model 1910 in .380 ACP used in the Sarajevo assassinations. © Heeresgeschichtliches Museum, Vienna.
D   Archduke Franz Ferdinand's military tunic worn on the day of the assassination. © Heeresgeschichtliches Museum.
E   The replica torso used for the final experiment, with the final armour around the shoulders ready to be buttoned up. © Royal Armouries.
F   The final vest fitted to the experimental torso before the experimental shots were fired. © Royal Armouries.
G   The final vest in the chronograph before the experimental shots were fired. © Royal Armouries.
H   The vest after receiving the shots to the neck area, and below. © Royal Armouries.
I   The neck area of the Roma torso. © Royal Armouries.
J   The bullet from the second shot shown caught in the armour. © Royal Armouries.

ACKNOWLEDGEMENTS

Firstly I am deeply indebted to Sławomir Łotsyz, Professor at the Institute for the History of Science, Polish Academy of Sciences, Warsaw, for his patience, guidance and sharing his important research and advice on the work of Casimir Zeglen. I am also extremely grateful to André Horne of Eurofins Forensics (formerly LGC Forensics) for sharing his knowledge of hand-loading, whilst working tirelessly with me to achieve the desired muzzle velocity for these experiments. I would also like to thank André Botha for his assistance in testing the replica armour effectively; Kevin Morley, for his brilliant work on creating the replica vests and samples; Her Serene Highness Princess Sophie von Hohenburg for her guidance on the estate of her great-grandfather Archduke Franz Ferdinand; the late Tony Edwards for his invaluable assistance with historic muzzle velocities; Dr M. Christian Ortner, Director of the Heeresgeschichtliches Museum, Vienna, for providing information on the Sarajevo assassinations; Vladimir Dedijer for his advice on Franz Ferdinand's murder; Maciej Ciunowicz of the Polish Army Museum, Warsaw; and Chris Streek for photographing the action as it happened. This study was made possible owing to the funding and testing facilities provided by the Royal Armouries and the National Firearms Centre. Finally and by no means least I would like to thank my excellent colleagues at the Royal Armouries; Jacob Bishop (Image Librarian), Jonathan Ferguson (Keeper of Firearms and Artillery), Martyn Lawrence (Publishing Manager), Jonathan Morris (Display Technician), Peter Smithurst (Curator Emeritus), Mike Sterry (Firearms Technical Manager) and Henry Yallop (Keeper of Armour and Edged Weapons) whose help, guidance and support have made this research possible.

INTRODUCTION

Archduke Franz Ferdinand's assassination in Sarajevo on 28 June 1914 has long been regarded as the 'spark' that ignited simmering European tensions and plunged the world into the First World War.[1] Born in 1863 to Archduke Karl Ludwig of Austro-Hungry and Princess Maria Annunciata of the Italian kingdom of Naples and the Two Sicilies, his relatively-unencumbered circumstances changed dramatically in 1889 after the suicide of his paternal cousin, Crown Prince Rudolph. With no living male issue, the Emperor of the Austro-Hungarian Empire, Franz Joseph I, named his brother Karl Ludwig as heir. After the death of his father in 1896 Franz Ferdinand took a step closer towards the Austro-Hungarian crown as he was named heir presumptive. Many of his duties as heir involved diplomatic visits on behalf of the emperor, and with duty came the threat of assassination. During Franz Ferdinand's time as heir presumptive (1896–1914), it is estimated that no fewer than 34 successful assassination plots were carried out on high profile individuals in positions of power.[2] The 35th and 36th assassinations – those of the Archduke and his wife – were the most far-reaching of all.

In 2013, as part of my role in the Collections Department at the Royal Armouries Museum, I catalogued a series of Browning Model 1910 pistols. I noticed one of them was stamped with the serial number 19590,[3] meaning that it was the 516th weapon to be manufactured *after* the infamous Browning Model 1910 used by Gavrilo Princip to assassinate Franz Ferdinand. A difference of 516 may be difficult to evaluate, but given the mass manufacture of these pistols, the two objects were closely related: in all likelihood, they were in the factory just a few weeks apart.[4] The Browning is a small, seemingly insignificant weapon. Black in colour with a barrel measuring just 9 cm (3.5 in), it fits easily in the hand. Looking at the Royal Armouries pistol meant that I was looking at a weapon identical to the one which triggered the First World War.

This object was my own 'spark' for further research. Knowing the consequences of the Archduke's assassination, I had often wondered what would have happened if his murder could have been prevented. Would there have been a war at all? What of the events that followed – the Russian Revolution, Nazi Germany, the Cold War? An infinity of 'what ifs' surround the shots fired in Sarajevo that day,[5] although regrettably they can not be the subject of this book: as a firearms curator, I was more interested in the arms and armour available in 1914. If this really was the 'era of assassination' and I was holding the equivalent of the weapon used to murder Franz Ferdinand, could I also uncover any attempts to prevent similar killings? What of the primitive body armour available at the time? I wanted to know if these technologies had the capabilities to save his life.

Given the inherent threat of assassination to heads of state, royalty and government officials during the late 19th and early 20th centuries, high profile individuals would have

The New York Times.

THE WEATHER
Local showers today; Tuesday, fair; fresh, shifting winds, becoming northwest.

NEW YORK, MONDAY, JUNE 29, 1914.—EIGHTEEN PAGES.

ONE CENT

HEIR TO AUSTRIA'S THRONE IS SLAIN WITH HIS WIFE BY A BOSNIAN YOUTH TO AVENGE SEIZURE OF HIS COUNTRY

Francis Ferdinand Shot During State Visit to Sarajevo.

TWO ATTACKS IN A DAY

Archduke Saves His Life First Time by Knocking Aside a Bomb Hurled at Auto.

SLAIN IN SECOND ATTEMPT

Lad Dashes at Car as the Royal Couple Return from Town Hall and Kills Both of Them.

LAID TO A SERVIAN PLOT

Heir Warned Not to Go to Bosnia, Where Populace Met Him with Servian Flags.

AGED EMPEROR IS STRICKEN

Shock of Tragedy Prostrates Francis Joseph—Young Assassin Proud of His Crime.

Archduke Francis Ferdinand and his Consort, the Duchess of Hohenberg
Slain by Assassin's Bullets.

1 News of Franz Ferdinand's assassination, *New York Times*, 29 June 1914.

been wise to take precautions against potential threats. Various sources indicate that Franz Ferdinand did exactly this – specifically, that he owned a piece of silk body armour made by Polish priest-turned-inventor Casimir Zeglen.[6] It is also argued that he failed to wear this armour on the day of his assassination, probably due to the warm temperatures in Sarajevo.[7] Given that the merest hint of conspiracy to commit political murder caused distress and anxiety at every European court, it certainly seems likely that Franz Ferdinand would have taken every available option to protect his life and that of his consort.

Archduke Franz Ferdinand and the Era of Assassination is the account of my investigation into the capabilities of the silk bullet-proof armours available in 1914. It is an expansion of an original article based on research carried at the Royal Armouries and the National Firearms Centre.[8] It sets out the background of what I refer to as the 'Era of Assassination', and assesses the weapons that were available to, and favoured by, assassins of the period. It also investigates Franz Ferdinand's personal circumstances and possible motivations for wearing silk bullet-proof armour, and charts the progression of the work of Casimir Zeglen and his quest to create silk armour 'to serve as protection of life from murderous bullets'.[9] Finally and most importantly, this study incorporates the most recent findings of my original ballistic testing on replica 'Zeglen-type' silk bullet-proof body armour, which until now have been unpublished. These replicas were made faithfully to 19th-century patents and specifications created by Zeglen, and have been tested against a FN Browning Model 1910 in .380 ACP. Ultimately, I have sought to determine whether or not Archduke Franz Ferdinand's life could have been saved by a Zeglen-type silk bullet-proof armour. It is a question that has haunted generations.

ST VITUS DAY 1914

The sun rose early in Sarajevo on 28 June 1914. Similar to the preceding days, the Serbian national holiday of St Vitus Day was to be hot and sticky.[1] St Vitus Day, which marked the Battle of Kosovo (1389) after which the Serbs were reduced to vassals of the Ottoman Empire, was a potent reminder of Serbian national identity.[2] It was also a day of national resistance to celebrate the fact that, despite defeat, a Serbian knight had killed Ottoman sultan Murad I on the battlefield.[3] More than 500 years later, many Bosnian-Serbs were of the opinion that the 'fight for a greater Serbia' should prevail.[4] Given this delicate relationship between Serbia and her new overlord Austro-Hungary, it is almost inexplicable that Archduke Franz Ferdinand, Austria's heir to the throne, should choose to visit Sarajevo on that particular public holiday – the day about which it was written that 'every Serb vowed revenge against unwelcome foreign intruders'.[5] Already a day of high tension, it was to become dramatically more so.

The St Vitus Day visit involved the royal couple, accompanied by their entourage, travelling through the city by motorcade. Franz Ferdinand's first task was to deliver a speech at Sarajevo's City Hall. At 10 o'clock the royal couple's motorcade left Filippovic Barracks for the city, their route taking them along the Appel Quay, which ran parallel to the Miljacka River.[6] It is believed that travelling in the first vehicle were the mayor and the police commissioner of Sarajevo, followed in an open-topped car by General Potiorek, Governor of Bosnia, Franz Ferdinand and his wife Sophie.[7] Two more cars followed, 'laden with members of the royal entourage and local dignitaries'.[8] As the motorcade progressed, Muhamed Mehmedbašić and Nedeljko Čabrinović, members of the Sarajevo cell of the 'Black Hand', positioned themselves on the quayside near to the Cumurja Bridge. Founded in 1911, the aim of the Black Hand was the 'unification of all Serbs through terrorism rather than political propaganda', cultivated from the spirit of violent Balkan nationalism at the turn of the century.[9]

Mehmedbašić and Čabrinović were two of seven conspirators involved in the plot to assassinate Franz Ferdinand that day. Whilst Mehmedbašić and Čabrinović stood amongst the crowds, also along the quayside were Vaso Čubrilović and Cvjetko Popović, preparing to strike should their comrades fail. If their action was unsuccessful, still further along the quay towards the Lateiner Bridge waited Gavrilo Princip and Trifko Grabež, poised to attack. Finally, the organiser of the plot, Danilo Ilić, 'moved about (the quayside) attempting to find the best position from which to shoot, should a shot present itself'.[10]

By 10.15 the Archduke's car reached the first group of conspirators, but at the critical moment, Mehmedbašić froze, unable to act. Unlike his comrade, Čabrinović wasted no time and withdrew a bomb 'from his pocket, struck the detonator cap against a lantern post, and hurled it at the vehicle, aiming at the green feathers atop Franz Ferdinand's helmet'.[11] The driver, seeing the bomb hurtling in the direction of the royal couple, accelerated the vehicle, and the hand grenade bounced off the rolled-down canvas top of the Archduke's

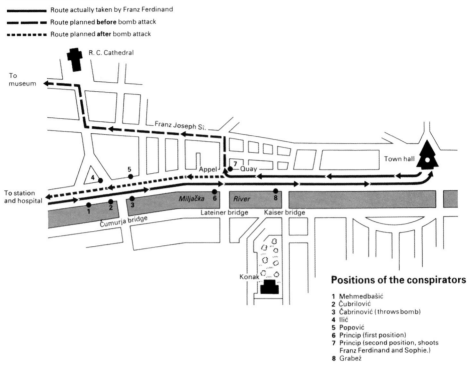

SARAJEVO 28th JUNE 1914

▬▬▬▬▬ Route actually taken by Franz Ferdinand
▬ ▬ ▬ ▬ Route planned **before** bomb attack
▪▪▪▪▪▪▪▪ Route planned **after** bomb attack

R. C. Cathedral

To museum

Franz Joseph St.

Town hall

Appel Quay

To station and hospital

Miljačka   River

Lateiner bridge   Kaiser bridge

Čumurja bridge

Konak

Positions of the conspirators

1 Mehmedbašić
2 Čubrilović
3 Čabrinović (throws bomb)
4 Ilić
5 Popović
6 Princip (first position)
7 Princip (second position, shoots Franz Ferdinand and Sophie.)
8 Grabež

2 Map of the Archduke's route through Sarajevo, 28 June 1914. © The National World War Museum.

car.[12] Several seconds later it exploded, injuring several onlookers as well as Colonel Merizzi, General Potiorek's aide-de-camp, who had been travelling in the car behind.[13] Čabrinović, unaware of the outcome of his actions, quickly jumped over the railings into the Miljacka River and plunged some 25 ft into the shallow riverbed.[14] As he made the jump he swallowed a cyanide pill, the precautionary measure with which all the conspirators had been issued, but the poison failed to act: it was either too weak or too old.[15] Located by the police, Čabrinović was pulled alive from the river and arrested.

The Archduke's car sped towards the city hall, and Franz Ferdinand turned to Potiorek and declared that 'he thought something like this might happen'.[16] His staff clearly felt uneasy: the Archduke's motorcade route had been published in the press and the possibility of a second attempt on his life could not be ruled out.[17] 'Do you think more attempts are going to be made on me today?' Franz Ferdinand asked Potiorek.[18] With the threat level raised, it was decided that the programme should be altered and the next location, the National Museum, be omitted. However, instead of retreating earlier than scheduled for lunch, the Archduke was adamant that he would visit Colonel Merizzi at the garrison hospital. The couple would drive back along the Appel Quay, the logic being that no one would expect them to pass that way twice. With the added protection of Count von Harrach travelling next to the Archduke, positioned on the running board of the royal couple's car, the vehicles set off down the quay on their ill-fated journey.

Unfortunately the driver of the first vehicle in the motorcade had not been told about the change of route. He turned right at the Lateiner Bridge on to Franz Joseph Street, and was followed by the Archduke's car. Realising the mistake Potiorek ordered the chauffeur to reverse back onto the Appel Quay.[19] With the car at a standstill as the chauffeur struggled to engage reverse gear, Gavrilo Princip (one of the third wave of potential attackers) approached and fired two shots from his Browning Model 1910 pistol, hitting the Archduke in the jugular and the Duchess in the abdomen.[20] Amidst shouts and screams, the royal couple's car raced to the Governor's residence. Count von Harrach, struggling to hold the Archduke upright, asked if he was experiencing any pain, to which the Archduke – still lucid – replied, 'It is nothing'.[21] Duchess Sophie, blood trickling from her mouth, was dead before the car arrived at the Governor's residence; carried from the car and laid upon a chaise longue, the Archduke died several minutes later. It was not yet 11.30 in the morning.

The late 19th century was a time fraught with threats of political assassinations that were unparalleled since the turbulent seventeenth century. This surge of unrest stood in dramatic contrast to the decades prior to the French Revolution, which had been an era of relative calm.[22] In Europe and North America, there was only one important politically-motivated murder – that of Peter III of Russia in 1762 – in the 120 years between the lynching of the De Witts in Holland in 1672 and the death of Gustav III of Sweden in 1792. During that time there were only two other attempts at assassination, by Robert-François Damiens against Louis XV of France (1757) and by two separate but apparently coordinated bands of gunmen against José I of Portugal in Lisbon the following year. (Both, incidentally, were travelling to or from appointments with their lovers.)

Following the French Revolution, assassination surfaced as arguably the most radical form of violent political protest in 19th-century Europe.[23] A steady trickle of killings (and

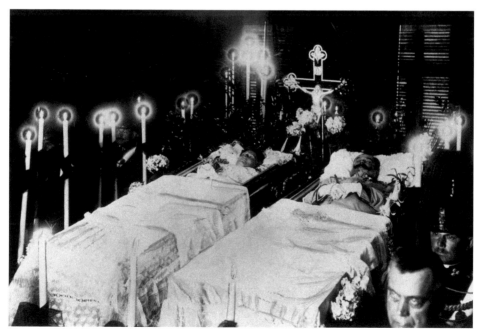

3 Archduke Franz Ferdinand and his wife Sophie Duchess of Hohenberg, lying in state in Vienna.
© Hulton Deutsch / Getty Images.

threats of killings), starting with British Prime Minister Spencer Percival in 1812, turned into a surging flood following the so-called 'year of revolution' in 1848. The middle years of the century witnessed a gradual collapse of the European balance of power established by the Peace of Westphalia (1648) and reasserted in 1815, and saw an era of rising nationalism as first Italy and then Germany asserted their independence. Two declining empires, Austrian and Ottoman, cast a lengthening shadow over Europe, and Serbia, lying at the fulcrum of these two extended territories and incensed at the annexation of Bosnia and Herzegovina in 1878, would form the seedbed of the trouble that led to Franz Ferdinand's killing.

Certainly regicide was nothing new to the royal courts of Europe. However, instead of courtiers jostling for personal power and the ear of the monarch, such acts now passed to radical political protestors who made dramatic attempts to upend the social order to achieve broader profound change. Nationalism, anarchism and nihilism became drivers of major change, with terrorism as a form of direct action – what the anarchists described as 'propaganda by deed' – being the most immediate way of rallying the masses.[24] The nationalist killing with the most far-reaching consequences was the work of the Serbian Black Hand movement in Sarajevo in 1914.[25]

Aside from the political ramifications, an attempt on a ruler's life cut to the very heart of their personal legitimacy. In an age when monarchs and chief ministers were expected to make ever-increasing public appearances, a king's presence amongst the 'common people' of his kingdom told of the mutual bonds between ruler and ruled: he was to appear in public unprotected and show before them all the trappings of power; they were to respect him and not molest his person. Assassination ran counter to this: in delegitimising the ruler, it simultaneously destabilised the established regime thus creating opportunities for more fundamental societal change.[26]

Notably, the later 20th century has seen a further shift. The nature of target selection by terrorist organisations has undergone a lengthy transformation in conjunction with the rise of mass politics and the development of new technologies that makes indiscriminate killing an increasingly prevalent political – and psychological – weapon. This book is written at a time when suicide bombs in markets and city centres raise terror alerts in large gatherings the world over. In the 19th and early 20th centuries, however, anarchist and terrorist organisations prioritised regicide. It was more important to subvert the legitimacy of the ruler than threaten the lives of ordinary citizens – who were, more often than not, hankering for change in any case.

In the late 19th century alone, assassins tried to kill almost every major European head of state. 1881, which saw Alexander II of Russia blown up by the *Narodnaya Volya* [People's Will] has been described as the 'inauguration of the era of regicides',[27] but in truth the half-century before 1914 saw plots against Emperor Franz Joseph of Austria, the Kaisers Wilhelm I and Wilhelm II of Germany, the Tsars Alexander II, Alexander III and Nicholas II of Russia, the kings Umberto I and Victor Emmanuel III of Italy, US President William McKinley and Great Britain's Queen Victoria. Nor, in this Indian summer of monarchical Europe, were prominent politicians safe: Italians were responsible for the killings of both French President Marie Francois Sadi Carnot in 1894 and Spanish Prime Minister Antonio Canovas del Castillo in 1897. In 1911, Prime Minister Pyotr Stolypin of Russia, who had survived several attempts on his life, was killed whilst attending a performance at the Kiev Opera House.[28] During the height of violence at the end of the 1800s, Friedrich Wilhelm, Crown Prince of Prussia, told one of his ministers that he greatly feared an attempt on his life: 'Whenever I get out of my coach I wonder whether the shot will come from the right or the left'.[29] It was into this political tinderbox that the assassination of Franz Ferdinand occurred, like a spark falling into a powder keg.

As a Hapsburg, Serbian nationalists saw Franz Ferdinand's presence as a constant reminder of the annexation of Bosnia. In order to resolve the existing tensions between the Slavic people of the Austro-Hungarian Empire and the house of Hapsburg, on his succession the Archduke planned to reorganise Austro-Hungary into a triple monarchy. His plan would grant the Slavic people of the empire 'equality'. This not only enraged other independent Slavic nations, but also alienated the more conservative-minded subjects of the Austro-Hungarian Empire.[30] The proposal of a triple monarchy may have provided just cause for other would-be assassins, yet it was not the Black Hand's rationale. Franz Ferdinand was more interested in maintaining Vienna's precarious relationship with Moscow than provoking a negative reaction from Sarajevo: he was not directly responsible for the injustices Princip and his fellow nationalists saw, and his removal would not bring about a radical change in regime.[31] Nevertheless, his killing went to the heart of the radical nationalist ambitions in this era: it was hoped that his murder would draw attention to the Black Hand's cause against what it saw as oppression from Vienna.[32]

Franz Ferdinand's assassination triggered a feverish reaction amongst the European powers.[33] Telegrams, letters and communiqués of every kind flew back and forth between St Petersburg, London, Paris, Berlin and Vienna; in a few short weeks, the old world would come crashing down. In Munich, a 25-year old Austrian artist by the name of Adolf Hitler wrote that 'a sense of impending catastrophe became transformed into a feeling of impatient expectance'.[34] In Sarajevo, meanwhile, the focus was on the killer. Assassin Gavrilo Princip's account of his notorious shots from the Browning Model 1910 pistol first stated that he had 'deliberately aimed at the Archduke'.[35] As this shot killed the Archduke, it would be tempting to assume that Princip was a proficient assassin. Yet Princip had only previously practised with the pistol in Belgrade one month prior to the assassination.[36] It has also been suggested that within organisations such as the Black Hand, 'marksmanship training was very limited as ammunition was both scarce and expensive'.[37] This therefore calls into question Princip's experience with this pistol. In stressful situations, only seasoned users of firearms are able to accurately account for their point of aim and the number of shots taken. If Princip was unfamiliar with shooting this model of pistol, he would have found it extremely difficult to direct his shot as intended. I have shot this particular pistol many times, and have found that the added safety on the grip must be completely depressed in order for the pistol to work. It requires a tight grip which can affect the user's aim.

In drawing from my own experience of shooting the Browning Model 1910 pistol, it is more likely that Princip seized the moment, pressed the pistol firmly into his hand and shot at random in the direction of the Archduke's car. This aligns with his second testimony: 'Where I aimed I do not know'.[38] In addition to his confusion neither could he remember how many times he had fired the pistol. Originally he thought he fired twice, but later during his testimony added 'perhaps more, because I was so excited'.[39] The lack of clarity in Princip's second account was most likely due to the high levels of adrenaline running through his body at the time he took his shots, making this account more plausible. Gavrilo Princip did achieve notoriety that day, but not for his own cause: instead, one of the luckiest shots in history ignited the fuse that plunged the world into total war.

WEAPONS OF CHOICE

Despite the different reasons and motivations for committing political murder, one aspect that remained the same for assassins during this period was the type of weaponry available.

EDGED WEAPONS AND EXPLOSIVES

Given the continuing development and availability of firearms in the early 1900s, it is tempting to assume that assassination by edged weapon would have been confined to the annals of history. Although not as common as firearms in assassination attempts, they were still used. In 1905, Theodoros Deligiannis, Prime Minister of Greece, was stabbed to death outside the Greek parliament. Almost eight years later, farmer Virgilio Mulatillo attacked the president of El Salvador, Manuel Enrique Araujo, with a machete.[1] Araujo's failed attempt to stabilise the economy prompted Mulatillo and his accomplices, Fermin Perez and Fabian Graciano, to act.[2] Araujo, who had been attending a concert at the San Salvador Bolivar Park, died five days later from his wounds.

The Hapsburgs themselves were no strangers to attempts on their lives, and had previously been the victims of both failed and successful plots involving edged weapons. In 1853, as the then-youthful Emperor Franz Joseph I watched troops being drilled in Vienna's Kärntnerbastei, a young Hungarian tailor, János Libényi, attacked the emperor with what was believed to be a kitchen knife.[3] It was resisted by the thick collar of Franz Joseph's military uniform, causing a small but deep wound in his back.[4] Libényi's purpose as a Hungarian nationalist was to separate the dual monarchy of Austro-Hungary in an attempt to give Hungary its independence,[5] echoing the cause of the Black Hand 60 years later against Hapsburg oppression. Although this event occurred before Franz Ferdinand was born, he would probably have been aware of it.

He would certainly have known of the misfortune that struck the Hapsburg family in 1898. The death of Empress Elisabeth of Austria, wife of Emperor Franz Joseph I and aunt to Franz Ferdinand, was a major tragedy for the family. Disappointed that his intended victim, Prince Henri Philippe Marie d'Orléans, had cancelled his visit to Geneva, Italian anarchist Luigi Lucheni instead decided to murder a different royal figurehead.[6] As the Empress walked along the shores of Lake Geneva to board a steamship Lucheni stabbed her in the chest with a needle file. Believing she had merely been punched, the Empress managed to board the ship before collapsing, whereupon it was discovered that the file had pierced both her heart and lung.

Towards the end of the 19th century the impersonal method of killing with explosives had become commonplace in assassinations. This method of assassination continued into the 20th century, as was seen with the Black Hand's failed attempt on Franz Ferdinand's

Plate A Top: Spanish Velo Dog revolver in 5.5 mm (XII.6996). Bottom: Spanish Velo Dog revolver in 6.35 mm (XII.4839). Both examples date from the early 20th century. © Royal Armouries.

Plate B A presentation Browning Model 1900, with inlaid gold (PR.8689). © Royal Armouries.

Plate C The Browning Model 1910 in .380 ACP used in the Sarajevo assassinations. © Heeresgeschichtliches Museum, Vienna.

© Heeresgeschichtliches Museum

Plate D Archduke Franz Ferdinand's military tunic worn on the day of the assassination. The bullet's entry can be seen just below the collar. © Heeresgeschichtliches Museum.

4 The attempted assassination of Emperor Franz Joseph I, 1853 by J. J. Reiner. © Wien Museum.

life by hand grenade. Although the chaos created through throwing a hand grenade was at the heart of the anarchist manifesto, various political organisations also adopted these destructive methods.[7] It was a hand grenade thrown by the revolutionary socialist group Narodnaya Volya that killed Tsar Alexander II in 1881. In 1904 the Socialist Revolutionary Party assassinated Vyacheslav von Plehve, the Russian Interior Minister, by throwing a bomb into his carriage.[8] The following year, the same perpetrators again used explosives to assassinate Grand Duke Sergei Alexandrovich Romanov, former Governor General of Moscow, son of Tsar Alexander II, and uncle of Tsar Nicholas II.[9]

In addition to being regaled with accounts of assassination attempts on his family's lives, in 1906 Franz Ferdinand was witness to another attack. Whilst attending the wedding of his distant relation King Alfonso XIII of Spain, a hand grenade was thrown at the wedding

5 The assassination of Empress Elisabeth of Austria, 1898. © Print Collector / Getty Images.

procession. Alfonso and his bride, Princess Victoria Eugenie of Battenberg, granddaughter of Queen Victoria, survived the blast but several spectators were killed.[10] According to Hertha Pauli, author of *The Secret of Sarajevo*, although Franz Ferdinand 'had heard much about such attempts, successful or unsuccessful' this was his 'first encounter with assassination'.[11]

6 The attempted assassination of King Alfonso XIII and Princess Victoria Eugenie of Battenberg, 1906. © Hulton Archive / Stringer / Getty Images.

PISTOLS

As we have seen, assassination by edged weapon was a possibility during the 'Era of Assassination', as was murder by explosive. Yet firearms were more popular with assassins. After the murder of President Araujo by machete in 1913, the remaining five assassinations that year would take place with firearms.[12] By the early 1900s, the pistol (or 'handgun') had become a popular method of assassination. Pistols during this period were classified as either 'revolvers' (from 'revolver pistol') which became common in the latter half of the 19th century, or by the 1890s the 'self-loading' pistol, though this took some years to become popular. The most basic distinction between the two is that a revolver holds its ammunition in a rotating cylinder, whilst a self-loading pistol feeds from a magazine (usually housed in the grip). As a class of weapon designed to be carried on the person and used one-handed, both were relatively compact and concealable. They could also be kept in a jacket pocket should the assassin prefer an attack at close-quarters, though they might have proven difficult to draw quickly.

For centuries the handgun has been praised but also 'reviled as a hopeless medium-range man stopper'.[13] The 'generic' effective range of a handgun is difficult to determine,[14] as there are many variables to consider. These include the type of powder used, the weight of the ammunition, the skill of the user and the type of handgun (whether revolver or self-loading pistol), to name but a few. In most circumstances, however, it is reasonable to suggest that the effective range that can be applied to a handgun is around 10 m.[15] Therefore the need to try and optimise the performance of the handgun during the late 19th and early 20th centuries gave birth to a range of technological advancements in pistol design, such as the development of the self-loading pistol. This brought more advanced pistols into the arena of assassination. Although more expensive to purchase, the self-loading pistol provided its user with more favourable odds. This was because most revolvers only chambered six rounds compared to the seven or eight available in most self-loading pistols. Now assassins had an all-important 'buffer' when seeking to kill. Even if they failed to hit their target, the self-loading pistol was quicker to reload than the traditional revolver – providing, of course, that the assassin had prepared in advance a fully-loaded spare magazine. The spare magazines were also a compact size and would have fitted comfortably into a jacket pocket.[16] A traditional 'single-action' revolver could be accurate, but had to be cocked before each shot, slowing down a would-be assassin. The self-loading pistols featured a similar trigger mechanism, but in the process of self-loading also self-cocked. This retained accuracy, sped up the firing process and made it more consistent. Faster firing revolvers did exist, but had heavier 'double-action' triggers, so called because pulling them automatically raised the hammer (the first action) by means of a mechanical linkage before dropping it again to fire (the second action).[17] They required much more effort to pull and disturbed the firer's aim significantly, as well as slowing down the rate of fire.[18] To a would-be assassin and their intended victim, these relatively minor technical points could mean the difference between life and death.

Traditional revolvers would also lose pressure due to the lack of a gas seal between the cylinder and the barrel (known as 'cylinder gap'). This loss of pressure affects the muzzle velocity at which a projectile can travel as it exits the muzzle,[19] therefore reducing its effective distance to the target. This flaw, although fractional, is reduced in self-loading pistols, because the pressure is contained within the locked breech. This is, however, only a minor disadvantage at close range. From 1892–5, Belgian firearms designer Léon Nagant sought to overcome this problem by patenting the first gas-sealed revolver, the only one of its type to triumph on the commercial market. The first 20,000 Nagant Model 1895 revolvers were manufactured in Liège. Having worked with the Russians on the Mosin Nagant Model 1891 bolt action rifle, Léon and his brother Émile had a close connection with the Russian military. This led to the official adoption of this revolver as its sidearm. Mass manufacture began at the Tula Arms Factory around 1898. The Nagant was originally available as double-action, and was issued to military officers and the police.[20] However, the Tsarist government ordered that some Model 1895 revolvers be retrofitted with single-action triggers and issued to enlisted men.[21] Due to the Nagant's design requirements, this revolver chambered an unusual, long-cased round with a tapered mouth fully enclosing the bullet, known as the 7.62x38mm Nagant. When cocked, the cylinder moved towards the barrel, closing the gap between the cylinder and barrel (Figure 7). As this movement occurs, the cartridge case neck is pressed into the hollowed rear of the revolver barrel, enhancing the gas seal system, thus increasing the velocity of the bullet by maximising the gas pressures from inside the cylinder. There is no doubt that the gas seal works effectively, but the resulting increase in velocity is minor, and justifies neither the extra layer of complexity nor the additional cost of manufacture. Furthermore, although this marginal improvement may have been desirable for military users wedded to the revolver, the much greater increase in velocity resulting from more potent cartridges soon rendered it moot. The gas seal would have enabled the use of a sound suppressor for clandestine attacks, something not possible with conventional revolvers. However, compatible suppressors were not available until the 1930s.

7 The Nagant Model 1895 (PR.7967). Note the gas seal located on the rear of barrel. © Royal Armouries.

8 The same weapon. When cocked, the gap between the gas seal and cylinder is closed. © Royal Armouries.

The Nagant Model 1895 revolver was rumoured to have been the weapon used in one of the most infamous assassinations of the 20th century: that of Tsar Nicholas II's shaman-cum-confidante, Gregory Rasputin. After pastries and wine thought to have contained 'enough cyanide to kill several men instantly' had no effect, he was apparently shot, beaten and drowned in a frozen river. Various contemporary revolvers have been suggested as the murder weapon, in particular the British Webley Mk VI in .455 in.[22] Theories suggesting British involvement in the murder have also surfaced, but as Douglas Smith points out, it was 'not only Englishmen who carried Webleys during the war'.[23]

The revolver remained the favoured criminal weapon, being cheaper, easier to purchase, and for the time being at least, more reliable. It was a pocket version of this weapon that was used in 1913 in yet another attempt on the life of King Alfonso XIII of Spain, as the *Timaru Herald* reported:

> An Attempt – the third – was made on King Alfonso's life yesterday in Madrid (states the London 'Daily News'). His Majesty was returning from a review, and was passing the Bank of Spain, when a man fired a pistol at him. The King, with splendid coolness, reined in his horse suddenly at the very moment the miscreant fired, and the bullet, instead of hitting him, struck the horse.[24]

The weapon in question was a type of pocket revolver known as a Velo Dog, which had been purchased in Madrid (Plate A).[25] A true Velo Dog revolver housed a slender long-case cartridge created by Parisian gunsmith Galand in 1894,[26] known as the 5.5 mm Velo Dog. Originally designed as a form of defence for cyclists against dog attacks, by 1900 they were widely available throughout Europe, particularly in Belgium, France and Spain.[27] Most Velo Dog pistols had an enclosed hammer (though this was not mandatory)[28] and a folding trigger, meaning that they did not snag on clothing when they were taken quickly out of a pocket. Gradually, other small pocket revolvers in different calibres also became known as Velo Dogs, although unfortunately it is not clear from the newspaper source which type or calibre was used in the attack on King Alfonso XIII.

Earlier the same year King George I of Greece was not so lucky. Alexandros Schinas assassinated the King with what was reported to be a 'heavy revolver',[29] whilst he took his afternoon constitutional towards the town of Thessaloniki in the company of his aide. As the King appeared from around a corner:

> The man on the bench rose and took a step or two forward; he put his hand to his breast pocket, drew a heavy revolver and fired it at the King's back at a distance of less than a yard. The bullet entered at the left side of the spine, penetrated the heart, and was afterwards found in the linen. The King collapsed as though struck by lightning, fell on his knees and then on his face.[30]

This close-quarter method of attack was chosen by many assassins of the early 20th century. During the assassination of King Umberto I of Italy (1900), the perpetrator, Gaetano Bresci, struck whilst his victim sat in his open-top carriage after leaving a presentation ceremony. Umberto, who had survived earlier attempts on his life in 1878 and 1897, was targeted at close quarters whilst sitting in his method of transport, as was Archduke Franz Ferdinand in 1914:

> Umberto stepped into an open carriage, ready to return to the royal villa. He saw a friend in the crowd and stood up to wave. Bresci fired four shots. 'I don't think it is serious' were the king's last words.[31]

The technique of Umberto I's murder was thought to have been the inspiration for the assassination of US President William McKinley in 1901.[32] McKinley's assassin, Leon Czolgosz, concealed a .32 calibre Iver Johnson 'safety automatic' revolver (Figure 9) under a handkerchief, and shot the president twice as he shook hands with visitors at the Pan-American Exposition in Buffalo.[33] Writing in *Collier's* Magazine, eyewitness to the McKinley assassination, John D. Wells, reported that 'suddenly I saw a hand shoved towards the President – two of them in fact – as if the person wished to grasp the President's hand in both of his own. In the palm of one hand, the right one, was a handkerchief. Then there were two shots in rapid succession.'[34] One shot hit the president in the breastbone and the other in the

9 The Iver Johnson 'Safety Automatic' revolver, 1895 First Variation – First Model (PR.4873). The same model of revolver was used in the assassination of President William McKinley. © Royal Armouries.

abdomen; a small piece of the president's clothing was also discovered in the wound four days after the shooting.[35] It was removed immediately, but six days after the assassination attempt, McKinley died from heart failure.[36] This assassination highlights the complications related to gunshot injuries during the early 20th century. Although the initial shot did not immediately kill the intended target, wounds were not always successfully treated and could result in the victim's death some days afterwards.

AN INTERNATIONAL RACE: THE DEVELOPMENT OF SELF-LOADING PISTOLS

The race for the optimum self-loading pistol design would take place around the turn of the century between the continents of North America and Europe. In North America John Moses Browning, one of the most prolific and influential firearms designers in history, designed his first prototype of a self-loading pistol in 1896, three years after the ground-breaking German Borchardt. Without the development of Browning's prototype (later named the Browning Model 1900), iconic self-loading pistols such as the Browning Model 1910 – used in the Sarajevo assassination – the Colt Model of 1911 and the Browning Hi-Power would have been very different. The same year that Browning produced his proto-type, Hart O. Berg of the Belgian firearms manufacturer Fabrique Nationale (FN), saw the potential of Browning's design. Berg invested in some of Browning's patents, as well as per-suading him to join his company.

Browning lived through a period of great innovation in firearms technology. Born in 1855 when modern self-contained ammunition did not exist, he lived to witness many of his designs being used during the First World War, before his death in 1926. Unlike his more iconic designs, the Model 1900 (Plate B) chambers the relatively weak .32 ACP (7.65x17mm SR Browning) cartridge, allowing it to employ the mechanically simple and reliable blowback mechanism.[1] FN eventually produced over 700,000 for sale to civilian, military and police customers.[2]

In 1904 Nikolay Bobrikov, the Russian Governor General of Finland, was assassinated by nationalist Eugen Schauman with a Browning Model 1900 pistol:

> *Eugen took out the pistol, aimed it with a shaking hand, and fired, hitting Bobrikov in the chest. Bobrikov took a step backwards, but remained standing. To Eugen's surprise the bullet didn't kill the governor. It hit a large brass medal on the governor's coat, ricocheted, and delivered a glan-cing blow to his shoulder … Eugen fired again, hitting Bobrikov in the neck. His third shot was to Bobrikov's abdomen. The governor-general flinched, but did not fall. He dropped his cane as he grasped at his stomach, his face showing only annoyance, not pain, at this assault.*[3]

This fictionalised portrayal of the event in John Canzanella's *Innocence and Anarchy* highlights the weakness of the Model 1900's .32 ACP round. After dramatically ricocheting off the brass medal, it took a shot to the neck and the abdomen to be effectual. In reality Bobrikov succumbed to his injuries, not only from two clean shots but from the third shot (aimed at his stomach) which hit his brass belt buckle, not a brass medal.[4] This caused the bullet to fragment and enter his body. This assassination has since given birth to populist theories about the type of bullet used by Eugen Schauman. Popular accounts state that Schuman used exploding bullets to carry out this assassination,[5] but the use of a hollow point bullet at first seems more likely than that of a bullet containing explosive material.

10 Inventor John Browning and Frank F. Burton, the Winchester expert on rifles, at the Winchester Plant, 1918. © US Army Heritage and Education Centre.

A hollow point bullet, named so due to its hollowed out tip, is designed to travel at a slower velocity and expands on entering the target. The impact causes the bullet to 'mushroom', thereby increasing its diameter, causing more internal damage to the target than, for example, a higher-velocity fully jacketed bullet. It could simply be a case of semantics and that the mushrooming effect has been misinterpreted here as exploding rather than expanding. That said, it is doubtful that a hollow point bullet for a Browning Model 1900 would have been commonly available in 1904.[6] Although populist sources suggest that Schuman was a pioneer of experimental hand loading,[7] it is technically doubtful that an improvised hollow point, or 'dum-dum' bullet,[8] made by Schuman would have cycled correctly in a self-loading pistol of that period.[9]

In light of these suggestions, it should be considered that an exploding bullet was used to assassinate Bobrikov. Along with being proficient in hand loading, Schuman allegedly experimented with mercury-filled bullets.[10] However, mercury alone would not explode and even if it entered the wound would be relatively harmless.[11] In this context 'mercury' may refer to mercury fulminate,[12] a compound originally used in percussion caps, alongside chlorate of potash, sulphur and charcoal. Percussion firearms of the early- to mid-19th century used percussion caps to ignite the weapons charge. These compounds and elements were ignited by the concussion of the firearm's hammer. For Schuman to make exploding ammunition he would have required a bullet with a cavity containing a very small amount of fulminate, and a striker that struck the fulminate when the bullet was stopped or seriously slowed down (such as when it strikes bone).[13]

Although theoretically feasible, it would have been complex to produce 'user friendly' mercury fulminate bullets. Due to the explosive nature of the improvised ammunition, in addition to it being filled with mercury fulminate, the risk to the user would increase. It was therefore more likely to explode in the hands of the assassin, rather than in the body of the intended victim. It could be that Schuman's intent was to poison Bobrikov using a mercury-filled bullet, rather than to create an explosion on impact by using mercury fulminate. It is possible that the use of mercury in this account has led others to interpret the bullet as exploding rather than poisonous. From rumours of chewed bullets[14] during the English Civil War,[15] to bullets boiled in garlic by the Mafia in the 20th century,[16] the poisoning of bullets feature frequently throughout the historical study of firearms. One of the first recorded assassinations by firearm took place in 1584, when it was rumoured that Prince William of Orange had been killed with poisoned ammunition.[17] The amount of mercury, however, in a .32 ACP round made by Schuman would have been relatively harmless. It would seem that the most likely explanation is that the bullet struck Bobrikov's belt buckle and caused the bullet to fragment. This fragmentation has been mistaken for an explosion. Furthermore, it seems that the association of mercury fulminate relied upon in earlier ammunition to cause 'an explosion' has been confused with the element mercury, resulting in the belief that this bullet was in fact poisoned.

As well as being used in various assassinations during the early 20th century, the FN Browning Model 1900 pistol was adopted as a standard service pistol by the Belgian military, at a time when lower-powered revolvers were the norm. Many countries did not adopt this pistol due to the size and perceived weakness of its cartridge. Combat experience around this time showed that a more powerful cartridge was needed to reliably penetrate heavy clothing and reach vital organs. In answer to this, in Germany, Georg J. Luger was tasked with redesigning the Borchardt C-93 (Figure 11), originally invented by Hugo Borchardt in 1893. Luger retained the successful mechanical aspects of the toggle-locked, short recoil design,[18] but made it much more compact and user friendly. The design was finalised and patented in 1898, and was first adopted in 7.65x21mm cartridge (derived from the Borchardt 7.65x25mm cartridge) by the Swiss in 1900. Meanwhile, Browning continued to refine his own blowback pistol designs, developing the Model 1903 which chambered the 9x20mmSR Browning Long cartridge. Although the Model 1903 was more powerful than its predecessor the Model 1900, Browning was eventually 'pipped to the post' when the definitive version of the Luger (Figure 12) entered service in 1908 (correctly designated the P08 Parabellum pistol) along with the equally famous 9x19mm Parabellum cartridge designed for and named after this pistol.

Browning's next instalment, the Browning Model 1910 pistol (Figure 14), still employed a simple blowback mechanism. Pistols using this system were more straightforward to produce but typically required cartridges with low velocities and pressures. As such they were more popular with civilian, rather than military, markets. The Model 1910 came in two versions, one developed for the .32 ACP (7.65x17mmSR Browning) cartridge and the other for the slightly larger .380 ACP (9x17mm Browning Short) cartridge, which Browning had developed for Colt in 1908. The .32 ACP version held seven rounds of ammunition and the .380 ACP version, used in the Sarajevo assassinations, held six. A few models were also designed with interchangeable barrels to accommodate both calibres, presumably designed for purchasers of the pistol who may have had ammunition availability issues.

Unlike its predecessors the Model 1900 and the Model 1903, the recoil spring of the Model 1910 was coiled around the barrel, rather than being located inside the slide. This was a feature of later blowback pistols such as the Walther PPK, and served to reduce the

11　The Borchardt C-93 (XII.3732), precursor to the P08 Parabellum Pistol. © Royal Armouries.

12　The P08 Parabellum Pistol, Serial Number 1 from Erfurt (PR.4154). © Royal Armouries.

13　The same weapon, with its toggle locked open showing the inside of the breech. © Royal Armouries.

14 The FN Browning Model 1910 in .380 ACP (PR.8687). This pistol is the same type of model used to assassinate Archduke Franz Ferdinand and his wife Sophie Duchess of Hohenberg. © Royal Armouries.

amount of component parts. The pistol also featured three safeties: a magazine safety that prevented firing when the magazine was removed; secondly, a grip safety that allowed the discharge of rounds only when the weapon was in the hand; and thirdly, a frame-mounted manually-operated safety catch. The pistol saw limited use in the Belgian military during the First World War,[19] mostly through private purchase, with the Model 1900 remaining as the standard-issue sidearm. After 1918 the Model 1910 was introduced into Belgian military service alongside the Model 1900. The two remained until the 1930s when both were replaced by the Browning Hi-Power.[20] With hindsight it would seem that the way forward for self-loading pistols was the short recoil system, but the toggle-lock system featured in the Borchardt and the P08 pistols was expensive and difficult to produce. For Browning after the Model 1910, work incorporating the short recoil system led to the development of his classic design, the Colt Government Model or Model of 1911. This iconic pistol became the classic sidearm of the US military, having only recently being withdrawn from service by its last remaining users, the US Marine Corps. It is still in use throughout the world by many other armed forces and remains a favourite amongst civilian users in the USA.

During this critical transition period from the end of 19th century, many self-loading blowback pistols were deemed unsuitable for widespread military use, but instead gained popularity with the civilian market. Although not seen as powerful and reliable enough for military use, in the hand of the early-20th century assassin they could still be deadly. Realising the danger inherent in their public personas, there is clear evidence that heads of state, and people in high office considered taking safety precautions: namely by contemplating the purchase of bullet-proof vests.

CASIMIR ZEGLEN: THE BULLET-PROOF PRIEST

The story of silk bullet-proof armour, made for the like of Archduke Franz Ferdinand, began in Chicago in 1893. Distressed by the assassination of Carter Harrison, the Mayor of Chicago, by a .38 calibre revolver, Polish-born priest-turned-inventor Casimir Zeglen (Figure 15) decided to devote the rest of his life to saving the lives of others.[1] Zeglen set about this task by developing a bullet-proof cloth, which harnessed the ballistic properties of silk. He developed and marketed this invention in the USA, tests for which began in December 1893 on what he proclaimed to be 'a product of great usefulness to the world'.[2]

Throughout history there have been many accounts of silk being used both accidently and intentionally as protection against weapons. Sławomir Łotysz, Professor at the Polish Academy of Sciences in Warsaw and a foremost academic on the life and work of Casimir Zeglen, has suggested various reasons for Zeglen's inspiration. Among these are accounts 'where silk fabric coincidently saved the lives of participants in revolver duels' in the USA during the 1880s.[3] Łotysz also suggests that Zeglen may have taken inspiration from further afield. 'Silk had already been adopted in China during the sixth and seventh centuries to quilt clothes used as protection against puncture wounds and cuts', eventually finding its way to Japan.[4] Known there as Kikou armour, with the added protection of outer metal plates, these armours were used by the Japanese until the 1870s.[5]

Unfortunately Zeglen never revealed the inspiration for his invention. It is possible that his idea for using silk in armour may have come after visiting the Chicago Columbian Exposition in 1893. Although there is no account of his attendance, he was a resident in the city at this time. A 'Japanese Pavilion'[6] was listed as one of the attractions at the Exposition.

> [Within this] fine educational exhibit, tinctured strongly with modern progress; silks and other textile fabrics; wonderful paper building materials; decorations and utensils; lacquered wares, swords, cutlery and other implements, and many other exhibits displaying rare scientific and artistic attainments are shown.[7]

Zeglen's idea for a bullet-proof cloth was eventually fashioned into silk armour, most commonly in the form of a vest, and by March 1897 he had received his first patents.[8] He continued to make improvements to the armour over the next few years, performing various experiments on his invention, testing the cloth against varying calibres, using both black powder and smokeless rounds.[9]

At first, Zeglen's experiments comprised of shooting at samples of fabric nailed to wooden planks.[10] Realising that a wooden post bore no resemblance to the human form, by June 1897 he progressed to wrapping his cloth around cadavers that he sourced from a Chicago dissection room: 'the body was fixed to the wall, and was held in an upright position with arms outstretched, while the torso was wrapped in the bullet-proof fabric'.[11]

15 Casimir Zeglen, inventor of silk bullet-proof armour. © The Library of Congress.

Buoyed by the interest his invention was beginning to attract, Zeglen was determined to go still further and test the fabric out on a 'live target'. One month later, in July 1897, Zeglen strapped his armour to a Great Dane before shooting several rounds at it.[12] History does not record the reaction of the dog, but, encouraged by its survival and finally confident with his invention, he began to test the cloth using himself as the target. After the first shot with a .32 calibre revolver Zeglen said: 'the concussion […] produced a temporary stinging sensation – that was all'.[13] Another shot, this time with a .38 calibre revolver, felt as 'someone had poked him in the ribs with his knuckles'.[14] It has to be concluded from the fact that Zeglen lived to tell the tales of these demonstrations that either his invention worked, or that he was a remarkable illusionist or charlatan.[15] As a result of these demonstrations his invention was endorsed by the Chicago police department, and would be later trialled by the US military in the early years of the new century.[16]

In late December 1897, however, Zeglen recognised the need for more consistent manufacturing methods. In order to mass-produce his invention and to make the product more effective, Zeglen entered a commercial partnership with fellow countryman and inventor Jan Szczepanik who produced a machine to manufacture the silk layer of the vest.[17] The partnership was turbulent owing to disagreements about the invention's ownership and it eventually fractured.[18] The split resulted in both men attempting to market bullet-proof armour: Zeglen worked primarily in the USA whilst Szczepanik focused his efforts on Europe.[19]

A frustrating gap in this otherwise fascinating story is the lack of contemporary evidence to prove that when worn by someone other than Casimir Zeglen, this type of armour successfully preserved the life of its wearer. Prince Obolenski, Governor of Kharkov, was reported to have been saved by Zeglen's bullet-proof armour after an assassination attempt in 1902. However, it has been suggested by Łotsyz that the bullets fired did not hit his torso and therefore the vest was not instrumental in saving him.[20] Interestingly Obolenski was not the only politician to have chanced upon Zeglen's invention. According to Zeglen and Szczepanik, many people in high-risk positions had already purchased these apparently life-saving vests. In 1902, for instance, Szczepanik stated in the *Chicago Daily Tribune* that the German emperor, the King of England and the president of France owned these types of armours.[21] Problematically, there is no substantive evidence of this and no testimony from the owners to confirm Szczepanik's claims. American president William McKinley is also thought to have been personally offered the garment, but unfortunately his secretary, George B. Cortelyou (ironically present at McKinley's assassination), had refused Zeglen's offer.[22] Clearly, advertising the ownership of such a garment was to be avoided,[23] as it would encourage would-be assassins to aim for the head rather than the protected torso. It is also entirely possible that these testimonies were mere marketing ploys.

One head of state who did take an interest in the invention was McKinley's successor President Theodore Roosevelt. Reported in the *Saint Paul's Globe* in September 1902, Casimir Zeglen stated: 'Mrs Roosevelt, wife of the president, has become interested in the bullet-proof cloth and during the coming visit of the president in Chicago this fall he will be given a personal inspection of its resisting qualities'.[24] Was this merely another marketing effort? It appears not. According to his personal papers, Theodore Roosevelt either received or wrote to Zeglen for pamphlets and a sample of his product.[25] Although there is no date or month on this document, Roosevelt became president in 1901 (the year of McKinley's assassination): it is more than likely that the request followed soon after the event that brought him to power. The correspondence is certainly evidence that Roosevelt and the White House were aware of Zeglen's bullet-proof cloth, and the statement in the *Saint Paul's Globe* the following year regarding his visit to Zeglen is therefore entirely plausible.[26]

Roosevelt's business link with Zeglen also suggests that the inventor may have been truthful in his interviews about the identities of his other clients. Zeglen named people whose lives were saved due to his bullet-proof armour in the Polish journal *Naokoło Świata*. 'As far as [Zeglen] knew', Archduke Franz Ferdinand was amongst this list of people to wear the armour, but as the conspirators directed their gun at his head not his chest, the armour was ineffective.[27] This suggests that Franz Ferdinand may have owned this invention, despite Zeglen not being absolutely sure in his testimony. The reason for this may be that the manufacturer of the Archduke's armour was Szczepanik not Zeglen, which is why Zeglen might not have been confident in confirming this report.[28] Regardless, no bullet-proof vest definitively owned by Franz Ferdinand has ever been found. This is surprising considering the number of other artefacts and personal effects preserved from the day of his assassination, to which we turn next.

THE CRIME SCENE

The 'Sarajevo' exhibition at the Heeresgeschichtliches Museum is dedicated to the story of the Sarajevo assassination. In addition to Gavilo Princip's pistol (Plate C) and the Gräf and Stift touring car in which the royal couple travelled that day (Figure 16), other objects linked to the assassination have also been put on display. These include the chaise longue on which the Archduke died, together with his uniform, which is now suspended above the chaise longue on a horizontal mount, given to the museum by his children (Figure 17).

The Browning Model 1910 pistol in .380 ACP was donated to the museum in 2004 by a Jesuit archive in southern Austria.[29] In 1914 a Jesuit monk, Anton Puntigam, had hidden it there at the outbreak of the war. Puntigam, who 'had given Franz Ferdinand and Sophie last rites, originally planned to set up a memorial to the couple, with the blessing of the family'.[30] In addition to the pistol, he had also supposedly taken other macabre 'souvenirs' from the royal couple. These included petals from Sophie's bouquet of roses and the bloodstained pillowcase from the chaise longue.[31]

Although this confirms the model of pistol used by Gavrilo Princip, the distance from which he shot the Archduke remains problematic. Following the Archduke's driver's wrong turn and subsequent reverse manoeuvre on Franz Josef Street, Princip shot the royal couple from the right-hand side of the vehicle at what is documented as point blank range.[32] Point blank range is often defined as 'less than four feet' (1.2 m).[33] However, the Archduke's position in the vehicle must also be considered. Historical accounts and evidence point towards Franz Ferdinand being sat on the left hand side, and thus furthest away from Princip. Judging by the width of the rear seats of the Gräf and Stift touring car (also held at the Heeresgeschichtliches Museum (Figure 16)) and the position of the Archduke, a reasonable estimate for the distance between Princip and Franz Ferdinand is 2 m. This is confirmed by the extent of the injuries sustained: the bullet that hit the Archduke entered around the right-hand side of his collarbone, severing his internal jugular vein before eventually lodging in his spine.[34] The evidence of the injury suggests that the shot was fired from approximately 2 m away.

But what of the Archduke's bullet-proof vest? If Franz Ferdinand had worn the Zeglen vest on the day he was assassinated, either the vest was not entirely bullet-proof (that is, it failed in its job), or it did not provide enough coverage to the neck area where the bullet struck

16 The Gräf and Stift touring car, donated by Count von Harrach. © Heeresgeschichtliches Museum, Vienna.

17 The Archduke's uniform. Note the slashed collar, chest area and left cut sleeve.
© Heeresgeschichtliches Museum, Vienna.

(that is, the bullet missed the vest altogether). Substantiating either theory is a problem due to the lack of a surviving bullet-proof vest from the scene. If indeed the Archduke had worn the vest whilst carrying out his visit, two scenarios present themselves: either it was incorporated into his military tunic, or somebody removed it from the scene.

The Archduke's surviving tunic is slashed diagonally across the chest, the gold collar slit and left sleeve cut, while the fading bloodstains around the throat and chest area are still visible. At first glance, it is difficult to tell whether the layers that make up the garment are those of contemporary body armour or merely a regular military tunic. However, the museum's director confirms that 'the original uniform of the Archduke corresponds to the normal, standardised uniform of a General of the Austro-Hungarian Army [...] the alleged body armor is a pure myth'.[35] Therefore the underlying layers of the tunic do not contain built-in silk armour. As the Heeresgeschichtliches Museum also owns the Archduke's undershirt (similarly soaked in blood), it is clear that if he had worn an integrated bullet-proof vest, it was entirely ineffective.

Having ruled out the theory of a built-in-armour we must return to the possibility of a separate garment which could be worn interchangeably. Contemporary newspaper articles claim that 'it was a well-guarded secret that the Archduke always wore a coat of silk strands which were woven obliquely so that no weapon or bullet could pierce it'.[36] The main problem in substantiating these sources is the lack of a separate bullet-proof vest, either with a bullet entry to the right side of the neck, or unworn in pristine condition. There is a slim possibility that the armour *was* worn on the day and later became separated from the rest of the assassination artefacts, although if this were the case it is surprising – given the media coverage of Puntigam's cache – that it has not yet emerged. By contrast, no irrefutable evidence can be found of an unworn vest since most of the family's items were destroyed during the First World War.[37] However, given Zeglen's testimony in the press and the inherent danger of public appearances for a person in Franz Ferdinand's position (as confirmed by the morning's repeated assassination attempts), it seems eminently plausible that the Archduke did at some point either considered investing in or did invest in Zeglen's invention. Therefore the effectiveness of this invention, regardless of whether or not it was worn in Sarajevo on 28 June 1914, opens up an intriguing avenue of modern arms and armour study.

PRELIMINARY TESTING

With the weapon identified, and the range of Princip's shot estimated at 2 m, one final element of testing my theory remained outstanding: if Franz Ferdinand did own a silk armour, which patent of Zeglen's was used to create it?[1] As the armour rumoured to have been owned by the Archduke has never been discovered, the patent designation remains a mystery. The most likely candidate for the Archduke's bullet-proof vest is Zeglen's last creation, *Patent 604,870* of 1898.

Zeglen's tests of the late 19th century were conducted with various revolvers of different calibre. Occasionally press reports detailed the manufacturer of the pistol used alongside the calibre of the firearm, such as 'former Chief of Police Applegate, of Dectaur [who] fired six shots at the dummy from a Smith & Wesson 38-caliber'. The model of revolver is on occasion omitted from these reports, so historical deductions need to be made. With the date of this report being 1902, it is possible that the cartridge used was a Smith & Wesson .38 Special (rather than the older .38 Smith & Wesson ammunition), but there is no conclusive proof to support this theory. In contrast, other reports stated the calibres used during the tests but not the manufacturers of the pistols themselves, such as this account from June 1897:

> The Chicago College of Dental Surgery filled with professors and army officers as a corpse dressed in 'Zeglen cloth' was brought forth. Count Zarnecki, a visiting Austrian army officer and an old friend of Zeglen's, did the honours with a .44 calibre [...] revolver. He drew a bead on the grisly target at 15 paces and fired.[2]

As this test took place in the USA in 1897, it could be deduced from the .44 calibre that the pistol used was the Colt Army Model of 1860 with Richards-Mason Conversion. Yet it cannot be discounted (although it is unlikely) that Zarnecki may have used his own Austrian army service revolver. During this period, the standard Austrian army revolvers in use were the Gasser Models 1870 and 1876, available in 11 mm calibres (or .44 inches, the calibre in question).[3] Our lack of knowledge as to the weapon that fired this .44 calibre projectile has its consequences, as the correct muzzle velocity of the mystery pistol cannot be determined; we therefore can not calculate the penetrative power withstood by the vest in 1897. Reports of the vest being able to withstand the (black-powder loaded) .32 Smith & Wesson round fired from a '32 Calibre Smith & Wesson revolver' do exist,[4] and from this it could be suggested the revolver used was the Smith & Wesson Model 1½. Again, however, this is only speculative. It is also worth noting that this calibre could have been reported incorrectly, and may have been the more recently-designed .32 Smith & Wesson Long, used in a different revolver. Other calibres used in Zeglen's tests included .38 Colt and .38 Smith & Wesson.[5]

The only way to establish if a Zeglen-type vest had the potential to save Franz Ferdinand's life was to test replica versions. In 2014 the Royal Armouries commissioned numerous sample squares and various full armours of two of Zeglen's patents (*Patent 577,999* and *Patent 604,870*). These were made by historical costume designer Kevin Morley of Accurate Originals and were created from Zeglen's patents and historical sources that came to light throughout my research. All of these were tested against the Browning Model 1910 pistol. As stated previously the Archduke would probably have purchased a Zeglen-type armour derived from Zeglen's last patent (*Patent 604,870*). However, in order to establish how Zeglen got to this stage of his design, in addition to understanding more about his methods of testing, I also decided to make and test samples of Zeglen's original armour, *Patent 577,999* (Figure 18). If this patent failed to withstand a shot and it was ever found

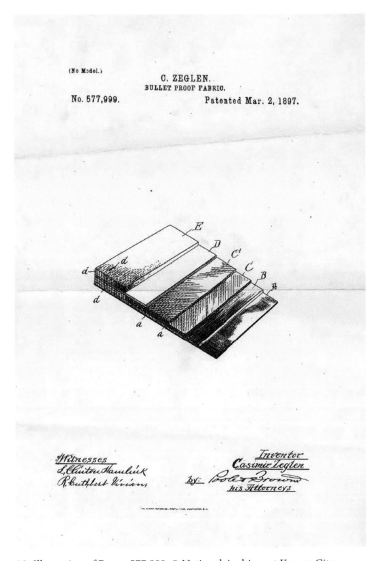

18 Illustration of Patent 577,999. © National Archives at Kansas City.

that Franz Ferdinand *did* have a vest made out of this material, then the probability of him surviving Princip's bullet would have been nil.

ZEGLEN'S PATENT 577,999

According to Zeglen, 'Layer A' illustrated on the patent's diagram is made up of the following materials:

> Designates the outermost layer of the fabric, or that against which the projectile strikes, said outer layer or covering consisting of two or more plies or thicknesses of a closely-woven, relatively heavy, strong fabric, such, for example, as canvas. After experimentation I have ascertained that the most satisfactory results are obtained by making this outer covering of linen canvas of a quality commonly known as 'Aberdeen' canvas, and while I recommend the same I do not desire to be limited thereto.[6]

My samples of this patent replicated Layer A with a standard layer of canvas. In addition to this, a further outermost facing of Melton wool was added on top of Layer A in order to replicate the military tunic of the Archduke which he wore on the day of his death. The annotation of the illustration continues with the description of Layer B:

> This layer B is relatively a thick layer, as shown, and may be composed of various kinds of hair. I have obtained the best results, however, by the use of the hair or, as it is more commonly called, the 'wool' of Angora goat, the hair of this animal having the desirable characteristics of strength, straightness, and fineness of staple, and being therefore susceptible of being formed into a very compact mass.[7]

A layer of unspun wool laid out flat (to replicate that of Zeglen's Angora wool) was used as Layer B in this patent's replica sample. Next, the somewhat complex description of the Layers C, C1 and aa:

> Next to the layer of hair, I provide a plurality of layers of strong flexible cords, threads, or strands C C1, the cords or strands of each layer being laid side by side or parallel with each other and directly in contact with each other and directly in contact with each other. The several layers C C1 of parallel-arranged strands are superposed one upon each other in such position that the several strands of one layer will lie in a direction transversely to or diagonally to the direction of the strands of the other layer, that is, at an angle to each other, as clearly shown in the drawing. In practice I have found that these woven inner layers are best constructed of, silk cord, which, owing to the fineness of the fiber and its relative great strength, and also, doubtless, to the peculiar characteristics of silk, afford the most to be limited thereto. The several layers thus formed are arranged, as shown, very compactly, and are secured together preferably by through-and-through stitching of silk thread, as indicated at aa, so that the whole becomes a hard and exceedingly compact mass having peculiar characteristics.[8]

Although difficult to interpret, Zeglen is referring to a complete layer of silk fabric. For the replica, a silk layer measuring 4 mm (0.15 in) in thickness, comprising layers of woven silk tightly sewn together and cut both on the bias and along the weave, were added as Layer C and C1. They were tightly compacted together by stitching, which replicated Layer aa. Finally, Layers D, E and d d which Zeglen transcribed as:

> A reinforcement D of pasteboard or analogous firm yet yielding material and inside of the reinforcement D and next to it I place a cushioning or relatively thick layer of felt E. The reinforcements or layers D E are secured in position in any suitable manner, but commonly, as shown in the drawing, by tacking or stitching d d, extending through the whole fabric.[9]

The replica Layer D of pasteboard (a type of cardboard, often used in the Victorian era to bind books) measuring 7 mm (0.27 in) in depth was added behind the silk layer as described in the patent. To finish, the back of the pasteboard layer was backed in felt and then lined in linen replicating the inside of a gentleman's waistcoat. Two replica sample squares and two replica armours were created as described above. The following summarises my earliest testing, conducted on the two replica samples.

TEST 1

Replica Patent 577,999 sample square versus Colt Model 1851 Navy Revolver in .36 calibre

Despite listing the composition of the vest, this patent does not give specific measurements of the protective layers, particularly that of the silk layer. With this being new territory the decision was made to conduct the first experiment with a lower-power black powder replica Colt Model 1851 Navy Revolver in .36 calibre (Figure 19). This more antiquated style of muzzle-loading type of firearm was selected because the charge could be reduced in the event that the round penetrated the sample. If successful the second sample would go head to head with the Browning Model 1910 pistol in .380 ACP – essentially, with the murder weapon itself.

The revolver was loaded with a 20-grain charge of FFg grade (medium grain) black powder,[10] which when choreographed produced an average muzzle velocity of 202 m/s (663 fps).[11] The projectile or ball weighed 80.63 grains and measured 9.5 mm (.375 in) in diameter. In order to secure the 30 cm x 30 cm sample squares in these preliminary tests, ballistic soap and gel were placed together and the sample was secured on to the front of the gel with bungee cords (Figure 20). This method would also catch any potential stray bullets, should the armour sample fail.

The Colt revolver was shot from a distance of 2 m. Remarkably, it failed to penetrate the sample (Figure 21 and 22), and on closer inspection (after dissection), it was found that the round had penetrated the first layer of Melton wool and unspun wool, but had lodged in the silk layer. These results showed that this patent could stop solid lead cylindro-conoidal bullets with a muzzle velocity up to 202 m/s (663 fps).

19 The replica Colt Model 1851 Navy Revolver in .36 calibre, about to be loaded for the test on the first sample.

20 The preliminary test set-up for testing sample squares of Zeglen's Patent 577,999. © Royal Armouries.

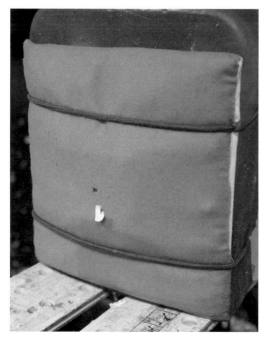

21 Bullet hole visible on the front of the sample. © Royal Armouries.

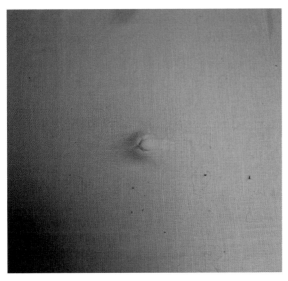

22 Rear of the sample showing the dent made by the round. © Royal Armouries.

TEST 2

Replica Patent 577,999 sample square versus Browning Model 1910 in .380 ACP

The next sample was tested against the Browning Model 1910 in .380 ACP. For this test modern .380 ACP ammunition was used. As with the Colt rounds, these were also chronographed to assess an average muzzle velocity, when used in conjunction with this particular pistol. Using 95 grain, full metal jacket .380 ACP rounds, the average muzzle velocity measured 262 m/s (860 fps), a full 60 m/s faster than the replica Colt achieved. Crucially, the modern .380 ACP ammunition was slightly more powerful than the 1914 loading, an issue to which we shall return. Given that this was a preliminary test based on the early patents, costly, time-consuming 'downloading' to achieve historic muzzle velocities would be carried out only if these initial results were encouraging.

The sample was secured as before and the Browning Model 1910 fired from 2 m. As expected the bullet penetrated the sample, clearly making its way through the 9 cm-thick ballistic gel and lodging in the soap after travelling a further 20 cm (Figure 23). The total depth of penetration compares favourably with the FBI's stated requirement for service pistol ammunition.[12] At the rear of the sample the third layer of unspun wool could be seen protruding through the innermost layer of linen (Figure 24).

23 The .380 ACP bullet fired from the Browning Model 1910 visible in the soap block located behind the sample of patent 577,999. © Royal Armouries.

24 The wool from the third layer having been dragged through to the innermost layer. © Royal Armouries.

Replica Patent 577,999, double-stacked sample squares versus the Browning Model 1910 in .380 ACP

Encouraged by the results produced by Test 1 against the Colt revolver, it was evident that the silk layer was resistant to lower velocity bullets. Therefore, in order to withstand a shot from a higher-velocity round, more layers of silk were required. In an impromptu experiment, using the two used samples from Test 1 and Test 2, the two were put together, one in front of the other (Figure 25).

   This meant that these samples were already compromised due to the previous rounds shot at them. Although Zeglen never used this method some creative licence was necessary – we have no evidence that he carried out any tests with a 20th-century self-loading pistol either. This test created a layer of silk measuring 8 mm (0.3 in). Secured and shot as before, the results were more encouraging. Although the .380 ACP again penetrated the first sample, the bullet was stopped by the layer of silk in the second sample (Figures 26, 27 and 28).

25 The two previously used samples secured together on the gel, with the soap block situated behind. © Royal Armouries.

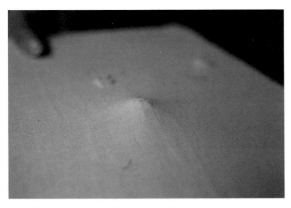

26 The bulge made at the rear by the sample retaining the bullet on the second stacked sample. © Royal Armouries.

27 The silk layer of the second stacked sample deformed after catching the bullet (after dissection). © Royal Armouries.

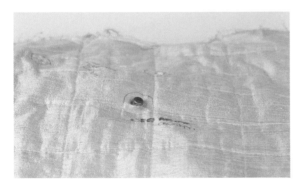

28 The .380 ACP bullet lodged in the silk of the second sample (after dissection). © Royal Armouries.

These preliminary tests confirmed the claims of Casimir Zeglen himself: that the 'fabric is bullet-proof'.[13] After the preliminary testing had taken place, it became apparent that this invention with additional silk layers could potentially stop a higher-velocity bullet from a .380 ACP round.

THE ZEGLEN BULLET-PROOF CLOTH CO. CATALOGUE

As exciting as it must have been to see Zeglen being shot at (and saved by his armour) during one of his live demonstrations, to make the maximum profit from his invention he needed to sell it. In order to do this he elected to advertise his invention to civilian, law enforcement and military markets. This could not be done through patents alone, and as we have seen, Zeglen's tests received much newspaper coverage. Yet for those interested parties who may have missed these reports, the details of the invention were also available in the Zeglen Bullet-Proof Cloth Co. catalogue (Figure 29).

This catalogue is a clever montage of newspaper articles reporting on Zeglen's tests, diagrams and customer testimonies. By 1897, Zeglen's armour had stirred the interest of the Chicago police department. Although it was not official standard issue, it gained notoriety within the force as individual officers privately purchased the armour for their own use. The catalogue from 1901 features an endorsement from Officer John Stupikowski of the 33rd Precinct, who stated:

> I hereby certify, that I have worn 'Zeglen's Bullet Proof Cloth' at different occasions and must say, that it gives perfect satisfaction. First of all it is so flexible, that it is worn without any inconvenience to the movement of the body. Besides having it on, you feel more secure and consequently it gives me courage to enter the most dangerous lurking places without fear. I would recommend it to all detective officers.[1]

Within the catalogue Zeglen writes about three different types of bullet-proof armours manufactured by the company, and describes the weapon type against which each would be most suitable. Most importantly he gives the measurements of the silk layers in his descriptions, an important aspect missing from his patents. The description for the 'first kind' (what later became known as the 'revolver armour') is as follows:

> The first kind of cloth, which resists bullets from revolvers, shrapnels and sporting guns, is made of silk thread, the whole composition being a textile fabric. The thickness of the cloth is one-fourth of an inch and weighs half a pound to the square foot. The fabric is soft and flexible so that all kinds of garments can be made or manufactured out of it. The most practical form of garment is a vest. This can be worn in all seasons of the year if desired, to serve as a protection of life, from murderous bullets, which up to the present have caused and cause so many deaths.[2]

The specification for the 'second kind', enhanced with additional silk layers, is described as follows:

> An inch thick and weighing two pounds to the square foot, and, as was stated above resists and wards off leaden bullets from military rifles at any distance; dum-dum bullets at a range of 800 yards. From this fabric, garments and devices for the protection of life can also be easily manufactured.[3]

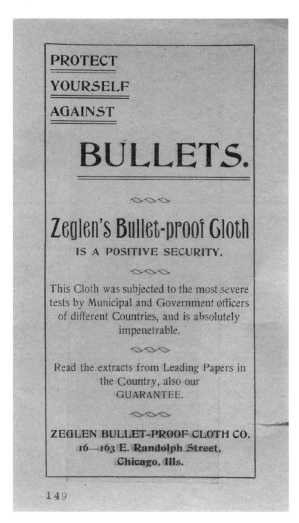

PROTECT

YOURSELF

AGAINST

BULLETS.

∞∞∞

Zeglen's Bullet-proof Cloth

IS A POSITIVE SECURITY.

∞∞∞

This Cloth was subjected to the most severe
tests by Municipal and Government officers
of different Countries, and is absolutely
impenetrable.

∞∞∞

Read the extracts from Leading Papers in
the Country, also our
GUARANTEE.

∞∞∞

ZEGLEN BULLET-PROOF CLOTH CO.
16—163 E. Randolph Street,
Chicago, Ills.

149

29 A page from Zeglen's Bullet-Proof Cloth Co. catalogue. © Library of Congress, Washington, DC.

Finally the 'third kind' or 'rifle armour' produced with the military in mind is described thus:

> *Bullet-proof fabric [...] made of silk, again being textile fabric, the thickness of which is one inch,
> covered on the outside by a steel armour of one sixteenth of an inch in thickness. The weight of the
> fabric is two pounds to the square foot and that of the steel armour two pounds to the square foot.
> Thus silk and steel together weigh 4 pounds to the square foot.*[4]

In addition to law enforcement testimonies and the accounts of how Zeglen wowed the
civilian world with his testing, the catalogue also includes selected reports of the armour's
performance in military trials. According to Łotysz, 'the fabric's resilience to rifle fire would
have been of particular interest to military men'.[5] After a couple of unsuccessful preliminary
tests involving the military with his 'revolver-resistant' armour, by November 1897 he had
finally presented his 'rifle-resistant' armour for official testing at the Springfield Armory in
Massachusetts.[6] This armour was reported to have been tested against the lead bullets of the
1873 Springfield Trap-Door, single shot rifle, in .45 in calibre.[7] It was then tested again with

an unspecified rifle. Contemporary newspapers reported this weapon to be 'a new-type of rifle with steel jacket bullets .30 in. calibre'.[8] It is entirely possible that this unrecorded rifle was from the Krag–Jørgensen family of rifles in .30–40 Krag, with the most likely candidate being the M1896 rifle that had just entered US service. To support this theory, the Zeglen Bullet-Proof Cloth Co. catalogue states 'Krag–Jørgensen guns used' and 'deadly steel bullets failed to penetrate at a distance of 200 yards'.[9] These statements are, however, questionable. Although the armour stopped the shots fired from the 1873 Springfield Trap-Door rifle, the Krag–Jørgensen's bullets pierced it from a distance of 300 yards.[10] Clearly if it could not stop the Krag–Jørgensen bullets at 300 yards, it could hardly have been successful at 200 yards. Łotysz in his account of the test adds that 'only when the marksman shot at the sample from 500 yards [with the Krag–Jørgensen] did the rifle fabric withstand the round'.[11] This distortion of the truth printed in this catalogue was probably due to Zeglen's belief that his 'rifle armour' would eventually work (most probably due to the steel layer) and that he needed to use his catalogue as a marketing ploy in order to stimulate sales.

With this military trial ending in failure in the USA, Zeglen had no chance of a recommendation to the Department of Defence. Ironically, the experiment had not been carried out properly: the armour sample was freely suspended, without any static backing, thus making the round more likely to penetrate the soft armour.[12] We also know that Zeglen knew this, due to his progression in trialling the armour with himself as the target. As the catalogue states 'improvements to be made',[13] it could be that these improvements were not made only to the invention itself, but also to the experimental materials and methods used in the demonstrations. The marketing of the armour's resistance to 'steel bullets' may also have been an attempt to attract investors – to a layperson, a steel bullet is sometimes perceived as a stronger (and thus more powerful) material than lead. This marketing ploy was misleading as both types of rounds used in the Krag–Jørgensen at that time had a lead core, jacketed in either steel or cupro-nickel.[14] Whilst the jacket of the bullet may be hard, it is also light and thin. A steel core, as used in armour-piercing ammunition, would have a higher density as well as hardness: it would keep its shape and penetrate more deeply.[15] In other words, a jacketed lead bullet would have a different enhanced penetrative power from a pure steel bullet. Theoretically, this ploy to market Zeglen's invention as 'modern steel' bullet-resisting armour could have changed the shape of wars to come.

Zeglen's military-focused marketing was evidently successful, as both Russia and Japan expressed an interest in the 'rifle' armour after an unsuccessful test carried out at Fort Sheridan in June 1897.[16] Interestingly at these trials Zeglen displayed his 'revolver' armour, as the 'rifle' armour was not ready until later that year for the trials at the Springfield Armory in Massachusetts.[17] Although the trials showed the effectiveness of the armour against revolvers, it failed – of course – against the Krag–Jørgensen rifle.[18] By all accounts, however, the onlookers were impressed by the idea of Zeglen's invention. By the spring of 1905, testing began at Gatchina, near St Petersburg, under the auspices of the Artillery Committee of the Russian army.[19] Four years following the circulation of the catalogue and with the Russo-Japanese War in full flow, Avenir Chemerzin, Captain of the Warsaw Citadel, paid Zeglen 30,000 rubles for the exclusive rights to his invention in the Russian Empire.[20] Although production for the Russians began in August 1905, Łotysz states that – rather than a typical vest – what was manufactured was more akin to a breastplate made of nickel-chromium steel plate.[21] He also suggests that 'the plate was covered with Zeglen's silk fabric, and lined with 15 mm of thick felt mat'.[22] Evidently Zeglen's fabric was not the bullet-repellent element, as a hardened steel plate of sufficient thickness would stop a rifle bullet regardless of cloth content. Given that peace was negotiated between Russia and Japan by

September 1905, we have to assume that this version of Zeglen's 'rifle' armour did not see enough military action for it to be properly field-tested.

From all this we can deduce one key thing. Had the Archduke purchased a vest for his public appearances, it seems most likely – knowing the specifications of Zeglen's various products – that it would have been the 'revolver armour' or the 'second kind' of vest. The 'rifle armour' can be immediately discounted for reasons relating to weight. Full armour (front and back inclusive) for a man of the Archduke's stature would require approximately nine square feet of 'coverage': given that a square foot of armour weighed 4 lbs (1.8 kg), this would have resulted in a total weight of around 36 lbs (16.2 kg). Furthermore, the inflexibility of the steel layer would have made the armour plainly visible to any would-be assassin, who would have changed their approach accordingly. By contrast, a 'revolver armour', even though it only 'provided protection from handguns and sporting guns',[23] remains a likely candidate, if for no other reason than the fact that revolvers were as prevalent as pistols or handguns during the 'Era of Assassination'. Having said this, it would have been useless against a rifled longarm, as Zeglen's military tests of the late 19th century clearly showed. That leaves the 'second kind' of armour. Although it was heavy (an estimated 18 lbs (8.16 kg) if worn by the Archduke), it was still half the weight of the more conspicuous 'rifle armour' and would have provided the maximum level of protection when balanced against manoeuvrability. It is the most likely potential life-saver of all the options available to Franz Ferdinand in 1914.

AIM FOR THE HEAD

The year following the Sarajevo assassinations a newspaper article reported that the Archduke was 'unfortunately shot in the head instead of the body'.[1] It is a notable claim in the context of this book, implying as it does that any bullet-proof vest would had been entirely ineffective. As it happens, it is also incorrect. The Archduke was shot in the jugular vein, just above the collarbone: the bullet's entry can be seen on the outside of his surviving tunic (Plate D).

The theory that Princip intentionally aimed for the Archduke's head served the Serbians well as a means to avoid war with Austro-Hungary. They proclaimed that the Archduke was 'a victim of a palace plot' to place suspicions on those in his closest circle, perhaps individuals who knew that Franz Ferdinand wore bullet-proof armour during public appearances.[2] The removal of the armour by palace officials, potentially to hide the evidence of this rumoured 'palace plot', made the headlines in 1915. Although possible, the claim is somewhat sensationalist. It is more plausible that Princip had been advised that if the chance arose he should aim for the Archduke's head, thus rendering any potential bullet-proof vest as irrelevant. Even so – and as previously discussed – Princip in all likelihood simply opened fire on the couple without aiming anywhere specific.

If Franz Ferdinand did own a silk bullet-proof vest, what would this garment have looked like? In the case of the Archduke, Casimir Zeglen's excuse for the failure of his invention was explained by the fact that 'the conspirator directed his gun at his head not his chest'.[3] Therefore a traditional 'crew-necked' style of Zeglen-type armour (which in most cases failed to adequately protect the neck area) would almost certainly have been ineffective (Figure 30). Furthermore, even if the bullet did touch the outer edge of the 'crew-necked' vest, the protection would likely have failed due to the edges of soft armour being notoriously weak. It is also possible that Zeglen's vague testimony was motivated by professional diplomacy, that is, that Franz Ferdinand *did* own a version of his armour, but that the manufacturer was Szczepanik not Zeglen.[4] Szczepanik may have claimed it as his invention, but his vests would have been made close to, if not exactly the same as, Zeglen's specifications and patents.

Correspondence with HSH Princess Sophie of Hohenberg, great-granddaughter of Archduke Franz Ferdinand, revealed that she was not familiar with the story of her great-grandfather's body armour, and 'if he did own such a piece it is no longer in the family's possession'.[5] Princess Sophie did suggest that it might lie in the collection at Konopiste Castle (one of the family's former residences), where the Archduke's vast collection of weapons and armour are still held. However, correspondence with the staff at Konopiste Castle confirmed no body armour exists there. With no physical example or irrefutable evidence that Franz Ferdinand owned Zeglen-type armour, I reverted again to further research

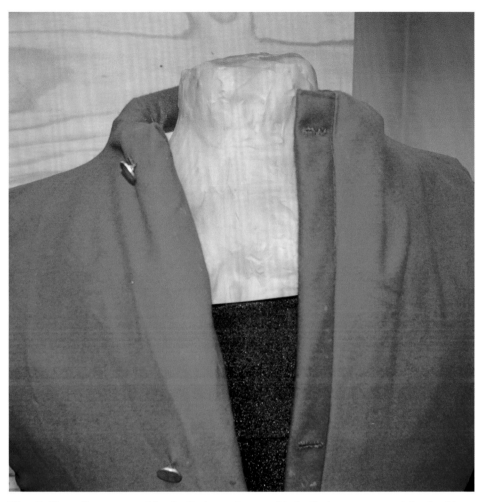

Plate E The replica torso used for the final experiment, with the final armour around the shoulders ready to be buttoned up. © Royal Armouries.

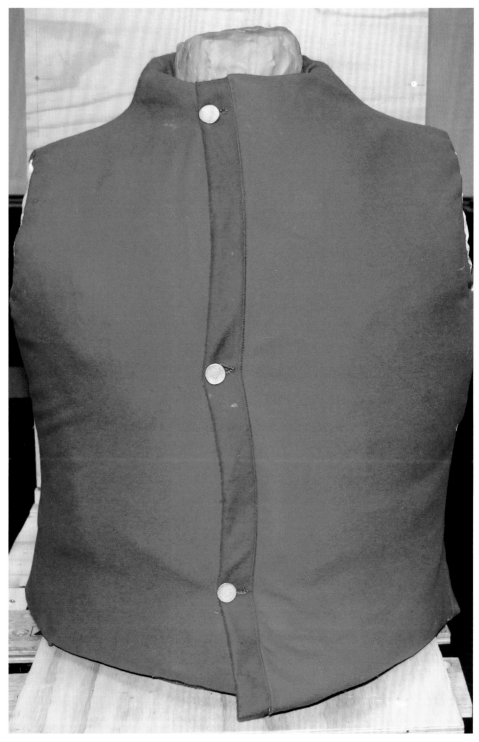

Plate F The final vest fitted to the experimental torso before the experimental shots were fired.
© Royal Armouries.

Plate G The final vest in the chronograph before the experimental shots were fired. © Royal Armouries.

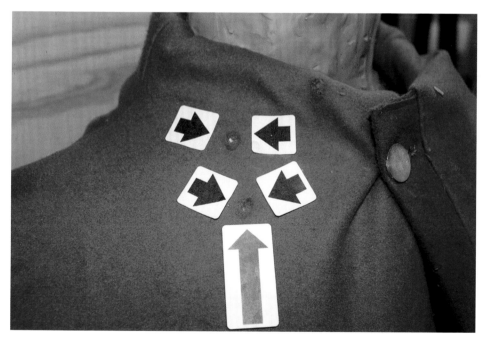

Plate H The vest after receiving the shots to the neck area, and below. The entry points of both bullets can be clearly seen. © Royal Armouries.

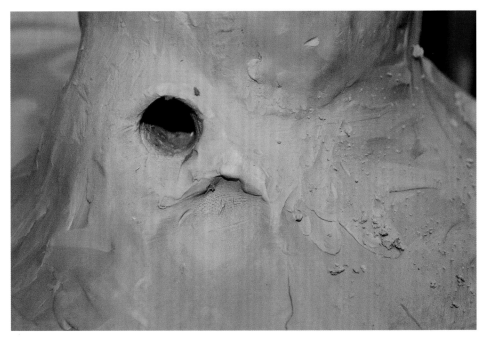

Plate I The neck area of the Roma torso. The shot replicating the Archduke's wound (top) shows that the bullet passed through the Roma. The dent 4 cm below shows where the second shot was repelled by the vest. © Royal Armouries.

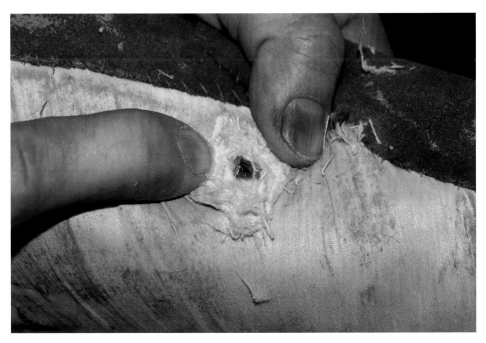

Plate J The bullet from the second shot shown caught in the armour. © Royal Armouries.

30 An example of Casimir Zeglen's 'crew necked' style of bullet-proof silk armour. © Library of Congress, Washington, DC.

on Zeglen's patents, and the possible demands of the consumer, to ascertain the requirement of different styles of bullet-proof vests.

To reiterate: if the Archduke did own a traditional 'crew-necked' bullet-proof vest, then in all likelihood the fatal shot would have struck just above it. However, if silk armours were available which provided coverage to the neck area, this extra protection would have increased a wearer's chance of survival if hit by a shot above the collar. Lest we forget, Franz Ferdinand was aware of such assassination attempts given the attempted knife attack on his uncle in 1853 (see second chapter, Weapons of choice). In addition to this attack, Franz Ferdinand may have been familiar with the details of the assassination of King Carlos I of Portugal, and his heir, Crown Prince Luís Filipe, that took place in Lisbon in 1908. The *Timaru Herald* reported that the King had been sat with his family in an open-top carriage:

> With a revolver in hand [the first assassin] rushed through the throng of spectators and jumped
> up behind the carriage and fired wounding the King on the left side. … He fired again, hitting the

*King in the back. King Carlos lifted his hand to his head then fell back in a state of collapse. …
Someone, probably a policeman, shot him dead [the first assassin]. … The leader of the regicides,
drew a carbine which was concealed beneath his cloak, moved towards the carriage and fired
twice, hitting the Crown Prince in the face. The man was about to fire again when a policeman
knocked up his arm and next a military officer killed the assassin with his sword.*[6]

What is interesting about this attack is the use of a carbine alongside a revolver. It was
stated in the same report that 'the assassins concealed five-chambered repeating carbines
beneath their cloaks'.[7] Although potentially misinterpreted as five *individual* carbines, it is
more likely this statement refers to one Winchester Model 1907 semi-automatic carbine
with a five-round capacity.[8] The press reported that the revolver bullets were 'still lodged in
the body' of the King, and that the bullets which hit the Crown Prince 'struck the sternum
and pierced the lung' whilst the other 'traversed his right check, emerging at the nape of
the neck'.[9] It is conceivable that the threat of assassination with 'modern' or more 'powerful'
weapons (such as the Winchester Model 1907 carbine) may have made potential victims
more fearful of the assassin's bullet, making bullet-proof armour seem an attractive invest-
ment. As such, armour which had the potential to resist both handgun and rifle rounds
could have been a profitable business endeavour for Zeglen. Although we can not tell if
the assassin aimed intentionally at the head of the Portuguese Crown Prince, this attack
highlights the vulnerability of the head and neck area. It affirms Zeglen's realisation that
protection of the neck area was vital if his armour was to be a success.

If the attempt on Franz Joseph I in 1853 indicated that reinforced collars could, in some
cases, offer protection from knives, it was clear that Zeglen's next move should be to devise a
collar that could withstand bullets. British Patent no. 5586 (Figure 31), dated 1897, displays
an illustration of his armour with a high-necked collar. In addition to this high-necked
patent, Łotsyz claims that 'high-necked versions of the vest were available at this time, espe-
cially in Europe',[10] making the existence of such armour plausible – and, critically, supports
my theory that the Archduke may have commissioned a high-necked design over the crew-
necked version.

TEST 4

*Replica British Patent 5586 high-necked vest versus the Browning Model
1910 in .380 ACP (silk layer 6.35 mm (0.25 in))*

In light of the discovery of *Patent 5586,* the Royal Armouries commissioned a full replica of
this high-necked armour to be built. This patent is the same composition of *Patent 577,999.*
This replica armour was given a 6.35 mm (0.25 in) layer of silk, to match the silk layer
description of Zeglen's 'revolver armour'. This was done because if the test was unsuccessful
the 'revolver armour' could be ruled out as not having the potential to save the Archduke's
life. Weighing 3.755 kg (8 lb 4 oz) the armour was bulky, very uncomfortable to wear, and
somewhat conspicuous, despite Zeglen's testimony that the vest 'can be worn in all seasons,
to serve as a protection of life, from murderous bullets'.[11]

After consultation with forensic expert André Botha, former Lead Reporter of Firearms
and Tool Marks at LGC Forensics, it became clear that an important requirement in soft
ballistic testing was to make sure the human body was replicated as accurately as possible.
Soft armour placed over a harder surface is more easily penetrated, owing to the supporting

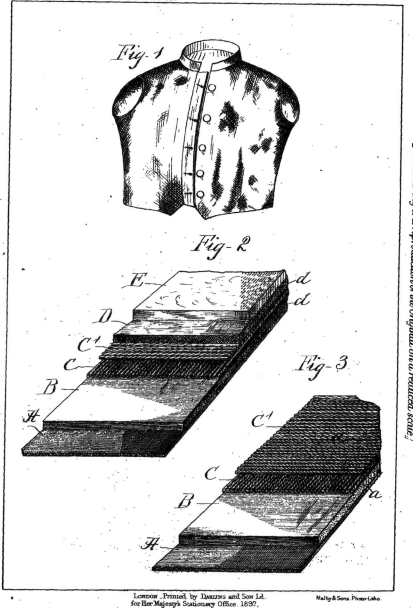

A.D. 1897. MARCH 2. N⁰. 5536.

ZEGLEN'S COMPLETE SPECIFICATION.

(1 SHEET)

Fig. 1

Fig. 2

Fig. 3

[This Drawing is a reproduction of the Original on a reduced scale.]

LONDON. Printed by DARLING and SON Ld.
for Her Majesty's Stationery Office. 1897.

Malby & Sons. Photo-Litho.

31 The British Patent 5586, illustrating the high-necked version of the armour. Image kindly supplied by Professor Sławomir Łotysz. 'Improvements in bullet-proof fabrics. Zeglen's complete specification. British Patent No. 5536, 2 March 1897. Accepted 3 April 1897'.

or 'shoring' effect of the rigid surface. A bullet-proof vest requires a softer backing material in order to absorb the energy of the projectile and thus resist the bullet. The principle is similar to that of a football net, formed by many long lengths of tether, interlaced with each other and fastened to the goal frame.[12] When a ball is kicked into the goal, it has energy in the form of forward inertia: it then pushes back on the tether lines at the point it hits the net. Since each tether extends across the goal frame, the energy is dispersed over a wide area instead of rebounding or bursting through the net. Similarly, when a handgun bullet strikes body armour, it is caught in a web of strong fibres which absorb and disperse the impact energy that is transmitted to the vest from the bullet.

This was something that Zeglen eventually took into account. Originally, as we have seen, he nailed his samples to wooden posts, which would have had a completely different reaction to the cadavers, live dogs and adult male (himself) who later wore the vests during his experiments. He likely did so in order to prove that it worked, but also to obtain maximum results from his invention.

When testing modern body armours, the majority of military and law enforcement agencies have settled on an oil/clay mixture for the backing material, known as Roma Plastilina.[13] Although harder and less deformable than human tissue, Roma Plastilina represents a 'worst-case scenario' backing material. The oil/clay mixture is roughly twice the density of human tissue, and does not therefore match its specific gravity. However, Roma Plastilina is a plastic material that does not recover its shape elastically. This is important for accurately measuring potential trauma through the 'back side signature', which is determined by means of a deformable backing material placed behind the targeted vest, should the vest not be penetrated.[14] An added advantage of using this mixture was the potential to measure the lethality of the bullet captured in the material, should it defeat the armour.

The Roma Plastilina was baked for 24 hours to replicate a human body temperature of 37 degrees Celsius. It was then placed into an oak mould and the armour secured in place around it with bungee cords. The depth of the oak mould measured 9 cm, with the Roma protruding over slightly at 10 cm in order to ensure it made direct contact with the armour. Extra Roma Plastilina was added to top of the oak mould in order to replicate the neck area. The diameter of the added neck area measured 5 cm. Would this test prove the success of Zeglen's high-necked body armour?

First to fire, the Browning Model 1910's .380 ACP round chronographed at 268 m/s (879 fps). Satisfied with the initial set-up, we placed a target on the vest's neck area, mimicking the location of the Archduke's entry wound. The shot was fired from a distance of 2 m. Slow-motion footage taken of this experiment captured the bullet in flight as it left the pistol's muzzle, entered the armour on target and exited at the back. On physical examination it was found that the round had indeed penetrated the neck area of this replica (Figures 32), travelled through the Roma 'neck', and continued its journey through the rear of the armour, exiting into the bullet trap. It was a failure.

With hindsight there were numerous reasons for the failure of Test 4. Firstly although the silk layer of the armour did cover the area where the Archduke was shot, it was still very close to the edge of the vest. This area is traditionally the weaker part of any soft armour. Second, the Roma did not replicate the Archduke's neck area sufficiently: in addition to supporting the area to be shot, we ought to have sculpted a full neck and shoulders so that the armour could sit correctly on the torso and absorb the impact of the shot – exactly as if it were worn by a human. Third, the modern loading of the .380

32 The high-necked replica version with bullet hole from the .380 ACP round clearly visible.
© Royal Armouries.

ACP round had a higher muzzle velocity than its 1914 counterpart, meaning that the modern ammunition was too powerful. Fourth, the sheer weight of this replica filled me with doubt about which patent the armours advertised in Zeglen's catalogue were built actually to. Finally it would seem that 6.35 mm (0.25 in) of silk was not sufficient enough to defeat the force of the early-20th-century self-loading pistol. If this invention was to work it was clear that we need not only an improved silk layer, but also to rectifying the testing conditions.

For all subsequent testing of sample squares, an oak box measuring 30 cm x 30 cm was used to house the Roma Plastilina, with samples again fixed to the front with bungee cords. This ensured the samples had direct contact to the ballistic equivalent of a human body. We also needed to ensure that the next test involving a full high-necked bullet-proof armour had suitable ballistic backing. This involved making a neck, part of the shoulders and breast area of Roma Plastilina. For the stomach and waist area, wood was carved into a torso shape with the clay mixture positioned on top of this stable platform. The wooden torso was then covered in Plastazote foam 'padding', so that the armour mirrored a human torso as closely as possible.

This was also the time for deeper research into the historic loading of the .380 ACP ammunition. The modern .380 ACP used in the previous tests differed slightly from its 1914 counterpart. Out of ten rounds the modern .380 ACP ammunition produced an average muzzle velocity of 262 m/s (860 fps) when chronographed. I turned for assistance to the late Tony Edwards, a great authority on the subject of historical ammunition, who believed that 'the earliest catalogue found listing the .380 ACP is the Eley Bros catalogue of 1912, which states a 95-grain bullet, but unfortunately no ballistics'.[15] Edwards believed that 'FN would also have been a candidate as they made the pistol [the Browning Model 1910] and their retailers would surely have stocked their ammunition'.[16] The oldest catalogue found by Edwards that includes the .380's ballistics was the Kynoch of 1925 which stated 'a 95-grain full jacketed bullet, produced a muzzle velocity of 840 fps'.[17] From this information, and no further evidence of a faster .380 ACP ammunition available from the beginning of the 20th century, I decided that the desired round for the rest of the testing would be created using a 95-grain full metal jacketed bullet, loaded to achieve about 256 m/s (840 fps). If it was found that this muzzle velocity was more powerful than it would have been in 1914, and the armour withstood the round, then it is safe to say that it would also have withstood Princip's slower bullet from the day of the assassination.

In order to 'download' the modern .380 ACP ammunition from 262 m/s (860 fps) to the 1925 loading of 256 m/s (840 fps), I enlisted the help of André Horne of Eurofins Forensics. Hand-loading ammunition is a time-consuming process. We had to shave metal off the full metal jacketed bullets to gain the desired weight of 95 grains and then remove flakes of powder to reach a propellant weight of 3.46 grains (which only after much chronographing was found to achieve the correct muzzle velocity for the type of nitro powder we were using). The process also required the re-crimping of the new bullets into the refilled casings.

By firing the downloaded ammunition from the Browning Model 1910 into the chrono-graph, the reading (the speed of the bullet) was picked up in the centre, and two speeds captured on these central cameras. The centre is located 2.67 m away from the pistol's muzzle. Twenty shots were fired during the downloading testing process and the average measurement of each camera calculated. The averages for each shot were added together and divided by two to find the average muzzle velocity, with these 20 totals in turn divided by 20 to determine the average of all rounds of downloaded ammunition. This was 254 m/s (833 fps). No ammunition batch ever produced is scientifically identical to another, but we were satisfied with the results achieved and decided that future ammunition would be loaded to 3.46 grains with the 95-grain full metal jacketed bullets. We would shoot from 4.67 m away, in order to account for the bullet reaching the 1925 muzzle velocity at the centre-point of the chronograph (2.67 m) plus two additional metres to account for the range from which Princip shot the Archduke. This, we had determined, was the 'point blank range' outlined in the sources (estimated between zero and 1.2 m) with an extra 80 cm given for the positioning of the Archduke in the car.

Having corrected the problem of ballistic backings, muzzle velocity and the dis-tance at which the experiments should be carried out, the next step was to adapt the amounts of silk used within the replica sample squares. With the failure of the previous testing of *Patent 577,999* containing 4 mm (0.15 in) silk and the high-necked *Patent 5586* containing 6.35 mm (0.25 in) silk, the obvious next step was to increase the silk layer to 25.4 mm (1 in) as specified in Zeglen's 'second kind' of vest. Without a physical sample of one of Zeglen's vests, we made the reasonable assumption that the Archduke would have chosen the most practical and efficient version available – a vest that provided sufficient protection but would not arouse suspicion and thereby tempt would-be assassins to aim for his head.

Professor Łotysz suggests that 'Zeglen may have wanted to discourage potential followers from plagiarising his invention, not trusting the effectiveness of the patent law'.[18] He claimed that by impregnating the fibres with a 'chemical solution which was known only to him',[19] he had managed to improve the ballistic capabilities of the armour. Furthermore, he continued to work on finding a proper method of arranging these strengthened fibres to make the fabric as strong as possible.[20] After numerous experiments, he finally elaborated on his special weaving method. In an interview for the *Washington Post* in September 1897 he referred to the final period of his work on the invention: 'in the end, thanks to a new weaving method and a new chemical, I have created a bullet-proof fabric as we know it today'.[21]

Until a sample of this armour emerges, the claim of a chemical strengthening agent cannot be discounted, but it would seem a bizarre move on Zeglen's part to exclude it. It would certainly have left him in a precarious position: if another inventor had managed to identify this chemical and work it into the armour, they would have been entitled to certain legal rights to this patent. I am in agreement with Łotysz: that this was a false claim on the part of Casimir Zeglen designed to deter other inventors. Furthermore, Zeglen may have known that the introduction of such a chemical could actually have weakened the armour's fibres. This theory is also supported by Zeglen's collaborative work on the armour with fellow Polish inventor Jan Szczepanik to introduce a new method of weaving to produce a more consistent, stronger product.

Although Zeglen could not have known the exact scientific properties of silk as they are known today, it is reasonable to assume that through his own experimentation, he believed that the key to his armour's bullet-resisting capabilities lay in the tensile strength of the silk layer. According to Łotysz:

> The tensile strength of the fibre is measured in centinewtons per tex (cN/tex) or grams per denier (g/d).[22] Raw silk withstands the force of 40–45 cN/tex. For comparison, various cotton species withstand 25–40 cN/tex.[23] The subsequent important property of silk is its relatively high elong-ation at break, which determines the material's stretch ability before it is torn. In the case of silk, this parameter is 18–25%, which explains why silk is more useful for a flexible vest than cotton (8%) or very inextensible flax fibre (3%).[24]

Zeglen's only option for increasing the ballistic capabilities of his invention would have been to add more layers of silk, hence his next two incarnations being the 'second kind' of bullet-proof fabric and his 'rifle armour'. My response was to increase my testing sample to 25.4 mm (1 in) of silk for *Patent 577,999*. If the 'second kind' of armour were to fail this would be the end of my experimentation.

TEST 5

Replica Patent 577,999 sample square versus Browning Model 1910 in .380 ACP (silk layer 25.4 mm (1 in))

Built to the same patent as the previous sample squares (the only difference being the increased silk layer), this example was the first to be tested against the downloaded .380 ACP ammunition, with its new average muzzle velocity of 254 m/s (833 fps), and at its new test distance of 4.67 m. After re-chronographing the ammunition to check that the muzzle velocity registered at the desired speed, the sample was fixed to the prepared box of Roma Plastilina and placed into position. Given the stage of the investigation, the pressure was immense. We knew that if this armour failed, the project would grind to a halt.

33 After dissection the head of the bullet is shown, visibly lodged in the silk layer. © Royal Armouries.

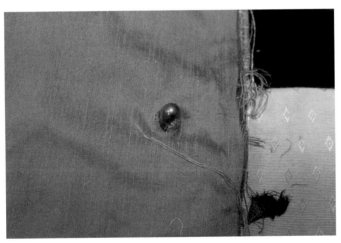

34 The second round lodged again in the silk layer of the sample. © Royal Armouries.

Two shots were fired, and we rushed to check. Remarkably this sample resisted both of the shots (Figure 33 and Figure 34). What we had discovered was immensely significant. It meant that an increased amount of silk was indeed the key to the success of Zeglen's bullet-proof armours. However, there remained a problem. The weight of Test 5's sample square, combined with its inflexibility, convinced me that a full vest made to this specification would have been impractical to wear. We resolved to push on.

PURE SILK

After examining the Zeglen Bullet-Proof Cloth Co. catalogue more carefully it became obvious that the replica samples and armours used in Tests 1–5 of *Patent 577,999* were not the same as those available for Franz Ferdinand to purchase. This was because they were not historically accurate representations of the type of Zeglen's silk armour available in *c.*1900. Zeglen stated that the whole composition is a 'textile fabric', a description not in keeping with the layer of 'pasteboard' found in *Patent 577,999*. Therefore this patent had to be disregarded with the focus switching to Zeglen's next patents, *Patent 578,000* (Figure 35) dated March 2nd 1897 and *Patent 604,870* (Figure 36) dated 31st May 1898.

Having studied *Patent 578,000* it is clear that this must also be disregarded as being the product described in the Zeglen Bullet-Proof Cloth Co. catalogue. Interestingly, *Patent 578,000* is notable in its own right for omitting the pasteboard layer from this invention. It still, however, includes the layers of Aberdeen canvas and Angora wool as the outermost layers with a silk layer on the inside. The loss of the felt backing and (more crucially) the pasteboard suggests that between *Patent 577,999* and *Patent 578,000* Zeglen realised how detrimental pasteboard was to his invention. The rigidity of such a material would have reduced the chances of the outer layers working effectively. Similar to nailing the fabric to a wooden post, a rigid backing such as pasteboard would create a 'shoring' effect, limiting the rearward movement of the fabric and therefore its capacity to absorb the energy of a projectile. Furthermore, the pasteboard layer would have limited the effectiveness of the Roma Plastilina to act as a 'football net' and absorb the bullet's impact. Through his testing Zeglen appeared to have realised this and omitted this troublesome layer.

With the next improved *Patent 604,870* coming to light at the same time as *Patent 577,800*, I deemed it unnecessary to build this patent, but proceeded to the later one. Through my testing I had drawn the same conclusions as Zeglen; the Canvas and Angora wool layers were not key ingredients to help these vests stop bullets. The key element was the silk.

It is most likely that *Patent 604,870* (Figure 36) is the specification to which the first and second vests advertised in Zeglen's catalogue were built, albeit with different amounts of silk. As seen with *Patent 577,800*, it also omits some of the original layers, but goes a step further leaving out Aberdeen canvas and Angora wool, being made predominantly from silk. In cross-referencing the diagram shown in the patent with Zeglen's written specification, the construction of this patent is as follows:

> *Layer A is designated as a cushioning layer and is placed in the inner side of the fabric or the side opposite that against which the projectile strikes. … In practice the layer A will usually be made of a thickness equal to about twice the thickness of layer B. … In practice I have found that both layer A and B are best constructed of silk.*[1]

From Zeglen's written specification it appears that 'layer A' acts as the cushioning between the torso and 'layer B'. The material used in 'layer A' is made up of 'layers of fine fibres either

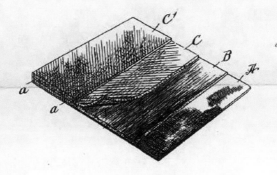

(No Model.)

C. ZEGLEN.
BULLET PROOF FABRIC.

No. 578,000.   Patented Mar. 2, 1897.

35 Illustration of Patent 578,000. © National Archives at Kansas City.

C. ZEGLEN.
BULLET PROOF FABRIC.

No. 604,870.   Patented May 31, 1898.

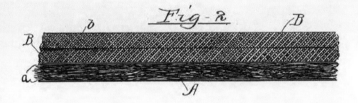

36 Illustration of Patent 604,870. © National Archives at Kansas City.

placed parallel with each other or in any manner and will be desirably confined within a covering or bag of silk'.[2] The bag of silk is marked on the patent as 'a'. Essentially, 'a' is a silk bag (like a cushion cover) containing what we would recognise as 'fine' silk cloth stacked in layers. Rather than being compressed together through tight stitching, they were placed on top of each other loosely in the silk bag.

The patent indicates that there could be two 'layer Bs'. These are the outermost layers 'against which the projectile strikes'.[3] Instead of being loosely placed inside a pouch, these layers are 'brought very compactly together and will be held very closely upon each other by their woven or braided construction'.[4] These layers of silk cloth were then stacked on top of each other, and compressed by being tightly stitched together. The 'b' on the diagram indicates the diameter of the silk chords used: Zeglen stated that 'the thickness of said layer B may be increased by making the strands "b" of greater diameter or by making this portion of the fabric of two or more separate layers as shown in Fig 2'.[5] Therefore if one did not have thick chords available, multiple layers of 'fine' silk cloth could be stacked on top of each other to create 'thick' silk cloth.

With the final Zeglen patent identified, and armed with the added advantage of the weight of the 'second' vest, I commissioned a sample square of *Patent 604,870,* with the silk layer and the weight conforming to Zeglen's second vest. Knowing that the layers contained within the invention were purely fabric, our replica sample was made almost entirely from silk, measuring 26.2 mm (1.03 in) in depth. The extra 0.8 mm in depth accounted for the Melton wool on the outermost layer, replicating the Archduke's tunic. The area of the samples measured 304 mm^2 (1 square foot) and weighed 0.90 kg (2 lb), as Zeglen had specified in his catalogue. The first layers (two layer Bs) were layers of woven silk fabric stitched together in two batches, so that two tightly compressed layers were created. Layer A was created with uncompacted layers of silk fabric, stacked on top of each other inside a silk pouch. This layer measured double the depth of the layer Bs. It was then finished with the Melton outermost face and backed with linen.

TEST 6

Replica Patent 604,870, sample square versus the Browning model 1910 in .380 ACP 'second kind' (25.4 mm (1 in) silk layer)

The same batch of downloaded ammunition was used for the test, and was chronographed at 257 m/s (843 fps). The distance of 4.67 m was again observed for the testing. The sample was attached with bungee cords to the box containing the Roma Plastilina, which had been baked for 24 hours to a temperature of 37 degrees Celsius. One shot was fired in the centre of the sample. The bullet travelled through the felt tunic (Figure 37) and through the first layer of tightly compacted silk layer B (Figure 38). The bullet then entered the second layer B of compact silk, before finally lodging in Layer A, the bag of loose woven silk, which acted as the cushioning layer nearest the body. It seemed that the compact layers of silk had managed to slow down the bullet considerably before the cushioning layer managed to stop it entirely. As we looked closely, we saw that the bullet had been retained in the fourth of 32 layers of woven loose silk (Figure 39).

This result was a remarkable moment in my investigation. I had shown that Zeglen's invention could not only stop low-velocity black powder bullets, but that it also worked against period ammunition as fired in self-loading pistols at the turn of the century. The final part of the jigsaw was ready to slot into place. For the ultimate test, I commissioned what I believe would have been Franz Ferdinand's vest of choice: Zeglen's *Patent 604,870* 'second kind' in the high-necked style of *Patent 5586.*

37 Bullet's entry can be seen on the outer face felt of the sample. © Royal Armouries.

38 The bullet's entry can be seen on first layer B of compact silk. © Royal Armouries.

39 The head of the bullet can be seen inside the contents of the silk pouch (layer 4 of loose woven silk), with its indentation captured in the next layer (layer 5), thus preventing penetration of the sample to the Roma Plastilina. © Royal Armouries.

FRANZ FERDINAND'S VEST?

After years researching and testing Zeglen's invention, the day arrived to test what I believed would have been the replica of Archduke Franz Ferdinand's silk armour of choice.

TEST 7

Replica Patent 604,870, Second kind of vest in the high-necked style of Patent 5586 versus the Browning Model 1910 in .380 ACP (1 in silk layer)

The ballistic backing for this experiment was as realistic as was feasibly possible. As previously discussed, a neck, shoulder and breast area was sculpted from ballistic clay, with the remainder of the torso made from wood and wrapped in Plastazote foam. The clay, baked again for 24 hours at 37 degrees Celsius, was positioned on the top (Plate E) and the vest was fitted to the torso ready to shoot (Plate F).

This final vest weighed 20 lbs (9 kg),[1] and was certainly not discreet. Putting it bluntly, it was incredibly bulky and heavy! Nevertheless, when compared to the earlier replica Zeglen armours, this vest remained flexible and allowed plenty of movement. Would Zeglen's manufacturing process have made the vest less conspicuous? Perhaps. Yet it would still have been big enough to make it obvious that its wearer was sporting something out of the ordinary. Even if my replica was tailored to the extent that Zeglen's inch thick armours would have been (and the weight reduced accordingly), I seriously doubt that Zeglen's version would have any less discernible.

Once again, the .380 ACP ammunition was chronographed and 15 shots were averaged at 254 m/s (833 fps). I decided that this vest should be shot twice, once in the neck area (to replicate the Archduke's fatal wound) and then centrally in the torso where the body armour is at its most protective (to give the armour a fairer test). The distance for the test was again 4.67 m from the muzzle of the pistol to the outside of the replica vest, but this time the shots were fired through the chronograph in order that their speed could be measured (Plate G).

The shots were fired. The first shot to the neck area registered at 255 m/s (837 fps), while the second, 4 cm lower, registered at 251 m/s (824 fps) (Plate H). These speeds could not have been any better for this experiment, and the fluctuations in muzzle velocity were as expected.

After the shot was taken and the range made safe, the rear of the vest was examined first, where it was found that *no bullets had exited the back of the armour*. The armour was then unbuttoned and removed to reveal the clay torso area. As the vest was gently removed, a bullet dropped from the garment. This was the bullet that replicated the Archduke's wound to the neck. As we moved to examine the clay torso, we identified a clear passage through the vest: the bullet had travelled deep into the clay 'neck' and was only stopped by the rear jacket collar (Plate I). However, the second bullet – fired just 4 cm below the fatal shot – had been caught by the armour (Plate J). This was a thrilling discovery, albeit one tainted by the knowledge that the shot that killed the Archduke was the higher shot to his neck. The illusive 'weak spot' located in the neck area on these particular types of fabric armours were clearly no match even for the weaker self-loading pistol rounds of the earlier 20th century (such as the .380 ACP). However, what we had established was this: although the like-for-like shot would almost certainly have been fatal, regardless of whether or not Franz Ferdinand was wearing a protective layer, the more obvious assassin's shot (to the chest/heart) may well have resulted in nothing more than a temporary wound – or even in the Archduke escaping entirely unscathed.

In many ways it is hardly surprising that the experiment was so close to throwing up a different result. Just as in the twenty-first century, body armour in 1914 was operating at the very limits of its capability: a shot to a weakened area of protection, whether it be Zeglen's silk armour or a modern piece of soft body armour, will almost certainly result in death. However, it is also true that just a few centimetres makes all the difference. Although we can say with confidence that Zeglen's *Patent 604,870*, the 'second kind' of vest in the high-necked style displayed in *Patent 5586*, would not have saved the Archduke's life on 28 June 1914, what we also know is that – had he been wearing a vest at all – he stood a reasonable chance of survival if only Princip's shot been 4 cm lower. Sophie, shot in the abdomen, would likely have lived too. What would have been the effect on European power politics of an *unsuccessful* assassination attempt? We can not say. On such fine margins empires stand and fall.

CONCLUSION

Casimir Zeglen's last public appearance with his invention took place in May 1913. Zeglen hung his armoured vest on a wooden board, which – after once again firing bullets from a .32 in calibre revolver – 'resembled a chunk of Swiss cheese'.[1] According to Łotysz, Zeglen blamed this experiments failure on the biodegrading of the vest's silk[2] – entirely probable, as organic material degrades over time. What is intriguing about this test is that Zeglen thought that there was a chance it might fail, since he reverted to hanging the sample on a wooden board (despite knowing the limitation of this approach) rather than wearing it himself. The choice of the lower-power calibre revolver, rather than that of a self-loading pistol, was also probably a conscious one, presumably in the hope that was enough strength in the armour to prevent the bullet penetrating. Why did he do this? Perhaps, having seen a finished replica of his armour, he decided that he needed to make the fabric more inconspicuous. Had he decided to trial different materials? What is plain is that he clearly did not yet believe in this incarnation of his invention, or he would have tested it on himself as he had done previously.

Nevertheless, this later episode should not detract from recognition of the genius of Casimir Zeglen. To discover the genuine historical accounts of Zeglen being shot at and surviving has been interesting, exciting and (at times) exhilarating. The practical ballistic testing has been equally important, particularly uncovering the surprising capability of this invention and its potential in protecting lives. In applying modern forensic science to a period body armour and evaluating different compositions, bullets, weapons and impact points, we have shown that Zeglen had indeed invented a viable form of personal body armour. The major barriers to creating effective bullet-resistant materials remained the cost and comfort, something which was to become a much greater challenge in the trenches of the Western Front.[3]

Part of this research is driven by the balance of probabilities. There is no concrete proof that the Archduke owned a silk bullet-proof vest, nor that the final vest (Test 7) would have been his preferred choice. However, a considered assessment of Franz Ferdinand's prominence during the 'Era of Assassination', together with an appreciation of the technology available to protect against an assassin's bullets, makes my conclusion eminently reasonable. I am quite certain that even if the Archduke did have a silk vest one inch thick, it would have been impossible to wear it comfortably during his visit to Sarajevo due to its sheer weight and bulk. It would also have been far too obvious. Furthermore, we know from the early tests that any vest with less than one inch of silk would have been ineffective against the newer self-loading pistols of the time (both in the neck area and elsewhere), regardless of how inconspicuous they may have been. We can categorically say that Gavrilo Princip's 'shot heard around the world' would still have been fatal even if Franz Ferdinand was wearing Zeglen's vest, although Duchess Sophie, if similarly protected, would have probably survived.

Casimir Zeglen moved on from bullet-proof vests to using his silk fabric as reinforcing cords in car tyres – something for which he received two patents.[4] His quest for a military contract for his bullet-proof armour was never realised. Due to its weight and the cost of mass production, his invention would never have been suitable to equip every soldier against the higher-powered firearms and ammunition being developed for use on the battlefield. Nevertheless, the opportunity to test his ideas have shown that the technology developed during the late 19th and early 20th century was indeed up to the job of protecting against the threat of an assassin's handgun. How many other politicians and heads of state had their lives saved by Zeglen's bullet-proof cloth? I hope that this study inspires a deeper interest in Casimir Zeglen and his forgotten silk armours amongst arms and armour scholars worldwide.

NOTES

INTRODUCTION

1 The historiography of the causes of the war is growing ever more immense, but one of the best accounts in the last 50 years remains Turner, L. C. F. 1970. *Origins of the First World War*, London. More recent works, chosen from an abundance of riches, are: Clark, C. 2013. *The sleepwalkers: how Europe went to war in 1914*, London; MacMillan, M. 2014. *The war that ended peace: how Europe abandoned peace for the First World War*, London; Stevenson, D. 2004. *Cataclysm: the First World War as political tragedy*, New York; Strachan, H. 2001. *The First World War, Volume 1: To arms*, Oxford. For a step-by-step account of the month following the assassination, see McMeekin, S. 2014. *July 1914: Countdown to war*, London.

2 Author's own statistical research.

3 The catalogue reference is Royal Armouries, PR.8687.

4 Actual production rates are impossible to calculate because records were lost when the factory burned down.

5 One recent counter-factual history that does entertain the 'what if' scenarios is Beatty, J. 2012. *The lost history of 1914*, London. See also Ferguson, N. ed. 1997. *Virtual history: alternatives and counterfactuals*, London.

6 Sources include: *New York Times*. 29 June 1914. 'Heir to Austria's throne is slain with his wife by a Bosnian youth to avenge seizure of his country', 1; Dean, B. 1920. *Helmets and body armor in modern warfare*, New Haven, 293; Dunston, S. 1984. *Flak jackets, 20th century military body armour*, Oxford, 4.

7 Dunston, *Flak jackets, 20th century military body armour*, 4.

8 Traynor, L. 2014. 'The Archduke and the bullet-proof vest: 19th-century innovation versus 20th-century firepower', *Arms & Armour 11.2*, 147–63. I am grateful to the Royal Armouries for permitting this material to be republished here. Readers should note that part of the research and testing in the article has been superceded by new material that appears for the first time in this book.

9 Washington, DC, Library of Congress, Manuscript Division, Series 14, reel 453, 150, 'Theodore Roosevelt Papers', n.d.

ST VITUS DAY 1914

1 Porter, L. 2010. *Assassination: a history of political murder*, London, 93; King, G. and Woolmans, S. 2013. *The assassination of the Archduke: Sarajevo 1914 and the murder that changed the world*, London, 197.

2 King and Woolmans, *Assassination of the Archduke*, 167.

3 McMeekin, S. 2014. *July 1914: countdown to war*, London, 5.

4 Mijatović, C. 1917. *The memoirs of a Balkan diplomatist*, London, 219–20.

5 Mijatović, *Memoirs of a Balkan diplomatist*, 219–20.

6 King and Woolmans, *Assassination of the Archduke*, 198.

7 Porter, *Assassination*, 93. There are various accounts of the number and sequence of cars in the procession, some of which are contradictory. Porter's information is derived from Massey, I. M. (tr. and ed.) 1953. *The origins of the war of 1914: Volume 2*, Oxford; see also Remak, J. 1959. *Sarajevo: the story of a political murder*, New York.

8 Porter, *Assassination*, 93; Massey, *The origins of the war of 1914*.

9 Porter, *Assassination*, 99.

10 Dedijer, V. 1967. *The road to Sarajevo*, New York, 313.

11 King and Woolmans, *Assassination of the Archduke*, 200.

12 Dedijer, *The road to Sarajevo*, 12.

13 Porter, *Assassination*, 93.

14 King and Woolmans, *Assassination of the Archduke*, 201.

15 King and Woolmans, *Assassination of the Archduke*, 201.

16 Smith, D. J. 2009. *One morning in Sarajevo*, London, 183.

17 King and Woolmans, *Assassination of the Archduke*, 200.

18 Dedijer, *The road to Sarajevo*, 14.

19 Porter, *Assassination*, 96.

20 Porter, *Assassination*, 96; McMeekin, *July 1914*, 20.

21 McMeekin, *July 1914*, 20.

22 Ford, F. L. 1976. 'Assassination in the eighteenth century: the dog that did not bark in the night', *Proceedings of the American Philosophical Society*, 120(3), 211–15. Ford is one of the few authors to have addressed assassination as a phenomenon in itself: his wide-ranging study is Ford, F. L. 1985. *Political murder: from tyrannicide to terrorism*, Cambridge, MA; although see Porter, L. 2010. *Assassination: a history of political murder*, London.

23 Hoffman, R. G. 2015. 'The age of assassination: monarchy and nation in nineteenth-century Europe', in Wachsmann, N. and Rüger, J. (eds.), *Rewriting German history: new perspectives on modern Germany*, London, 122.

24 Jensen, R. B. 2015. *The battle against anarchist terrorism: an international history, 1878–1934*, Cambridge, 16. More widely, see Hubac-Occhipinti, O. 2007. 'Anarchist terrorists of the nineteenth century', in Chaliand, G. and Blin, A. (eds.), *The history of terrorism from antiquity to Al Qaeda*, Berkeley, CA, 113–31; Dietze, C. and Schenk, F. 2009. 'Traditionelle Herrscher in moderner Gefahr. Soldatisch-aristokratische Tugendhaftigkeit und das Konzept der Sicherheit im späten 19. Jahrhundert', *Geschichte und Gesellschaft*, 35(3), 368–401. The earlier impact of the French Revolution on fantasies of terrorism and regicidal threat is discussed in Barrell, J. 2000. *Imagining the king's death: figurative treason, fantasies of regicide, 1793–1796*, Oxford; and threats to Queen Victoria and Prince Albert in Murphy, P. T. 2012. *Shooting Victoria: madness, mayhem and the rebirth of the British monarchy*, London.

25 Porter, *Assassination*, 93–111.

26 See discussion in Hoffman, 'Age of assassination', 127, and references there cited. For ritual and public performance in 19th-century Britain: Cannadine, D. 1983. 'The context, performance and meaning of ritual: The British monarchy and the "invention of tradition", *c*.1820–1977', in Hobsbawm, E. J. and Ranger, T. O. (eds.), *The invention of tradition*, Cambridge, 101–64; Plunkett, J. 2003. *Queen Victoria: first media monarch*, Oxford. For Prussia: Barclay, D. E. 1992. 'Ritual, ceremonial, and the "invention" of a monarchical tradition in nineteenth-century Prussia', in Duchhardt, H., Jackson, R. A. and Sturdy, D. (eds.), *European monarchy: its evolution and practice from Roman antiquity to modern times*, Stuttgart, 207–20. For the increasing numbers of royal visits abroad during the 'long' 19th century, see Paulmann, J. 2000. *Pomp und Politik: Monarchenbegegnungen in Europa zwischen Ancien Régime und Erstem Weltkrieg*, Munich.

27 Chaliand, G. and Blin, A. 2007. 'The "golden age" of terrorism', in Chaliand, G. and Blin, A. (eds.), *The history of terrorism from antiquity to Al Qaeda*, Berkeley, CA, 176.

28 Ternon, Y. 2007. 'Russian terrorism, 1878–1908', in Chaliand, G. and Blin, A. (eds.), *The history of terrorism from antiquity to Al Qaeda*, Berkeley, CA, 132–74; and more broadly, Geifman, A. 1993.

Thou shalt kill: revolutionary terrorism in Russia, 1894–1917, Princeton. Sebag Montefiore, S. 2016. *The Romanovs 1613–1918*, London, 532, notes that 3,600 Russian officials were assassinated between October 1905 and September 1906 as a result of Stolypin's crackdown on the rebels.

29 Quoted in Hoffman, 'Age of assassination', 127.

30 King and Woolmans, Assassination of the Archduke, xxxiii.

31 Porter, *Assassination*, 104.

32 Porter, *Assassination*, 104. Franz Ferdinand's assassination has also been compared to the disorder caused by the Comitaji, who 'were armed bands of Balkan Slav partisans or irregulars originally formed in Macedonia, whose aim was to cause mayhem and disorder in Ottoman lands in the Balkans and hasten the end of the Ottoman presence there'. See Roberts, I. 2016. 'The Black Hand and the Sarajevo conspiracy', in Anastasakis, O. et al (eds.) 2016. *Balkan legacies of the Great War: the past is never dead*, London, 32.

33 For example, McMeekin, *July 1914*, 23–86.

34 Quoted in David, S. 2014. *100 days to victory: how the Great War was fought and won 1914–1918*, London, 4.

35 Dedijer, *The road to Sarajevo*, 321.

36 Vanderlinden, A. 2013. *FN Browning pistols: side arms that shaped world history*, Greensboro, 24–5.

37 Vanderlinden, *FN Browning pistols*, 24–5.

38 Vanderlinden, *FN Browning pistols*, 24–5.

39 Vanderlinden, *FN Browning pistols*, 24–5.

WEAPONS OF CHOICE

1 Chasteen, J. 1984. 'Manuel Enrique Araujo and the failure of reform in El Salvador, 1911–1913', *South Eastern Latin Americanist* 28:2, 1–15 at p. 5.

2 Chasteen, 'Manuel Enrique Araujo', 7.

3 Österreichische Staatsarchiv. n.d. 'Attentat auf Kaiser Franz Joseph', www.oesta.gv.at/site/cob__41967/currentpage__0/6644/default.aspx (accessed 27 September 2016).

4 Österreichische Staatsarchiv. 'Attentat auf Kaiser Franz Joseph'.

5 Sacks, N. 2016. *WWI the causes*, Minneapolis, 76.

6 Jensen, *The battle against anarchist terrorism*, 138; Sisi Museum. n.d., 'Assassination', http://www.hofburg-wien.at/en/things-to-know/sisi-museum/tour-of-the-sisi-museum/assassination.html (accessed 27 September 2016).

7 Porter, *Assassination*, 104–5.

8 Porter, *Assassination*, 104–5.

9 Lincoln, W. B. 1983. *The Romanovs: autocrats of all the Russians*, New York, 651.

10 Jensen, *The battle against anarchist terrorism*, 301.

11 Pauli, H. 1966. *The secret of Sarajevo: the story of Franz Ferdinand and Sophie*, London, 203.

12 These were; President Francisco I Madero of Mexico shot along with Vice President José María Pino Suárez; Abraham González, provisional and constitutional governor of Chihuahua; Mahmud Şevket Pasha, Grand Vizier of the Ottoman Empire and King George I of Greece.

13 Hogg, I. 1979. *The complete handgun 1300 to the present*, London, 5.

14 Effective range is the range at which a target is hit whilst the bullet is still able to travel at high speed.

15 Ferguson, J. Personal correspondence, 10 December 2016.

16 It is worth mentioning that speed-loaders used for the simultaneous loading of a top-break or swing-out revolver cylinder were also available during this period. This device would have potentially increased the assassin's ability to reload.

17 Most double-action revolvers could also be manually cocked, however this reduced the firing rate to that of a single action weapon.

18 Most modern revolvers are traditional double-action, which means they may operate either in single-action or self-cocking mode. The accepted meaning of 'double-action' has, confusingly, come to be the same as 'self-cocking', so modern revolvers that cannot be pre-cocked are called

'double-action-only'. See Tilstone, W. J, Savage, K. A. and Clark, L. A. 2006. *Forensic science: an encyclopaedia of history, methods, and techniques,* Santa Barbara, 158–9.

19 Muzzle velocity is calculated as the speed a projectile travels at the moment it leaves the muzzle of a firearm.

20 Popenker, M. 1999–2018. 'Nagant m.1895', http://modernfirearms.net/handguns/double-action-revolvers/rus/nagan-arr-195-e.html (accessed 20 February 2018).

21 Popenker, M. 'Nagant m.1895'.

22 Smith, D. 2016. *Rasputin*, London, 631–2.

23 Smith, *Rasputin*, 632.

24 *The Timaru Herald*, 30 May 1913. 'Shots at King Alfonso', 9.

25 *The Timaru Herald*, 'Shots at King Alfonso', 9.

26 Zhuk, A. B. 1995. *The illustrated encyclopaedia of handguns,* London, 155.

27 Zhuk, *The illustrated encyclopaedia of handguns*, 155.

28 Friedman, J. 2017. 'What is a Velo Dog?' www.velodogs.com (accessed 20 February 2018).

29 Christmas, W. 1914. *The life of King George of Greece,* New York, 4746 (page reference from Kindle edition).

30 Christmas, *The life of King George of Greece*, 4746.

31 Duggan, C. (2007) *The force of destiny, a history of Italy since 1796*, New York, 349.

32 Jensen, *The battle against anarchist terrorism*, 57.

33 The conclusion has been made by the author from the images of the revolver used in McKinley's assassination. The murder weapon appears to be the 1895 First Variation–First Model, .32 calibre Iver Johnson safety automatic revolver. See The Buffalo History Museum. 2018. 'Collection Highlights', www.buffalohistory.org/Explore/Collections.aspx (accessed 20 February 2018).

34 Vulich, N. L. 2013. *Killing the presidents: presidential assassinations and assassination attempts,* USA, 60.

35 Jensen, *The battle against anarchist terrorism*, 239.

36 Vulich, *Killing the presidents*, 71–2.

AN INTERNATIONAL RACE: THE DEVELOPMENT OF SELF-LOADING PISTOLS

1 Several blowback operating systems exist for self-loading firearms. The broad principal of operation is 'a system of operation that obtains energy from the motion of the cartridge as it is pushed to the rear by expanding gases created by the ignition of the propellant charge.' See Chinn, G. M. 1955. *The machine gun, Volume IV. Design analysis of automatic firing mechanisms and related components*, Washington, 3.

2 Popenker, M. 1999–2018. 'FN Browning M1900', http://world.guns.ru/handguns/hg/be/fn-browning-m1900-e.html (accessed 20 February 2018).

3 Canzanella, J. 2010. *Innocence and anarchy*, Bloomington, 544.

4 Polvinen, T, 1995. *Imperial borderland: Bobrikov and the attempted russification of Finland, 1898–1904,* London, 259.

5 Kekkonen, P.T. 1999. 'ARCANE, or forbidden knowledge about handloading', http://guns.connect.fi/gow/arcane2.html (accessed 27 September 2016).

6 Ferguson, J. Personal correspondence, 12 October 2016.

7 Kekkonen, P.T. 1999. 'ARCANE, or forbidden knowledge about handloading', http://guns.connect.fi/gow/arcane2.html (accessed 27 September 2016).

8 Dum-dum, or dumdum, refers to a type of hollow point bullet named after an early British example produced at the Dum Dum Arsenal near Calcutta, India.

9 Ferguson, J., Personal correspondence, 12 October 2016.

10 Kekkonen, 'ARCANE, or Forbidden Knowledge about Handloading'.

11 Smithurst, P., Personal correspondence, 12 October 2016.

12 Smithurst, P., Personal correspondence, 12 October 2016.

13 Smithurst, P., Personal correspondence, 12 October 2016.

14 A chewed lead bullet would result in the ammunition becoming 'rough and/or infectious, or directly poisoned in some way'. See Ferguson, J. 2016. '"You Never Dreamt of a Poysoned Bullet": "Forbidden" ammunition from the 16th century to the present', unpublished conference paper at Firearms and the Common Law Tradition, Aspen Institute, Washington DC.

15 For an example of chewed bullets from the Siege of Colchester, see London, British Museum, 1519, 305, Capell & Lucas to Fairfax, Ellis's Original Letters, First series, Vol.III, MS. Donat, 1648.

16 The Mafia believed that 'garlic would induce gangrene into victims' wounds': Allsop, K. 1990. *The bootleggers and their era,* Chicago, 88. However, if anything, garlic is actually mildly anti-septic: Ferguson, J. '"You Never Dreamt of a Poysoned Bullet"'.

17 Motley, J. L . 1883. *The rise of the Dutch Republic: A History,* New York, 611.

18 Short recoil is one of several recoil operating systems used in self-loading firearms, which relay on recoil energy to cycle the action. These systems are categorised by how the parts of the weapon move under recoil. The barrel and bolt of short recoil weapons will only recoil together for a 'short' distance before they separate. Once the barrel stops, the bolt continues towards the rear, compressing the recoil spring which in turn performs the extraction of the spent case followed by the feeding of a new. Finally as the bolt returns forward it locks into the barrel pushing it back into place.

19 Vanderlinden, A. 2001. *The Belgian Browning pistols 1889–1949,* Greensboro, 120.

20 Vanderlinden, *The Belgian Browning pistols 1889–1949,* 120.

CASIMIR ZEGLEN: THE BULLET-PROOF PRIEST

1 *Quincy Weekly Whig.* 22 April 1897. *'New bullet-proof cloth invented by a priest in Chicago',* 2.

2 *Washington Post,* 26 September 1897. *'Bullet-Proof Priest',* 25.

3 Łotysz, S. 2014. 'Tailored to the times: the story of Casimir Zeglen's silk bullet-proof vest', *Arms & Armour,* Vol. 11 No. 2, 168.

4 Łotysz, 'Tailored to the times', 167.

5 Łotysz, 'Tailored to the times', 169.

6 Trumball, W. and Inglehart, W. M. 1893. 'The world's Columbian Exposition, Chicago, 1893 / a full description of the buildings and exhibits in all departments', https://archive.org/stream/worldscolumbiane00whit/worldscolumbiane00whit_djvu.txt (accessed 12 December 2016), 129.

7 Trumball and Inglehart, 'The world's Columbian Exposition', 129. In addition, 'armour exhibits' were also displayed, although it is difficult to ascertain the type or provenance of these armours. I would suggest that it was perhaps plate armour as it featured in the 'Implement Section', 181.

8 Łotysz, 'Tailored to the times', 169. Different patents for Zeglen's silk bullet-proof armour exist, as he fine-tuned his invention throughout the late 19th century. Of the two tested in this study, the patents illustrate the composition of the armours and state the materials used in the invention. All that is missing from these patents are details of the specific measurements of the layers (particularly the silk layer): Traynor, 'The Archduke and the bullet-proof vest', 154.

9 Traynor, 'The Archduke and the bullet-proof vest', 149.

10 Collins, P. 2005. 'The bullet-proof priest', *New Scientist,* 2496, 54.

11 Łotysz, 'Tailored to the times', 170.

12 *Los Angeles Times,* July 4 1897. *'Did not hurt a dog',* 7.

13 *Quincy Daily Journal,* 12 July 1897. *'Bullet proof cloth',* 2; Łotysz, 'Tailored to the times: the story of Casimir Zeglen's silk bullet-proof vest', 171.

14 Łotysz, 'Tailored to the times', 171.

15 Traynor, 'The Archduke and the bullet-proof vest', 149. Note also that if Zeglen was a charlatan, under loaded and/or frangible ammunition would be enough to fool many spectators.

16 Traynor, 'The Archduke and the bullet-proof vest', 149.

17 Łotysz, S. Personal correspondence, 19 February 2014.

18 Traynor, 'The Archduke and the bullet-proof vest', 149.

19 Łotysz, Personal correspondence.

20 Apart from recalling the example of Archduke Franz Ferdinand, Zeglen wrote: 'as far as I know, Turkish Sultan, Abdul Hamid, and Duke Oblonsky survived the attempts on their lives only due to having worn the bulletproof armours which I invented.' See, 'Od Redakcji', 1927. *Naokoło Świata 41*, 174–5. See also Łotysz, 'Tailored to the times' (note 102).

21 *Chicago Daily Tribune*. 22 September 1901. '*Underwear to protect monarchs*', 39.

22 *Washington Post*. 4 February 1904. '*Coat to protect president*', 11.

23 Traynor, 'The Archduke and the bullet-proof vest', 151.

24 *Saint Pauls Globe*. 15 September 1902. '*Bullet-proof vest*', 4.

25 The Library of Congress. 1969. 'Index to Theodore Roosevelt Papers', *Transcript*, Vol. 3 R-Z, 1321.

26 Traynor, 'The Archduke and the bullet-proof vest', 151.

27 'Od Redakcji', 174–5.

28 Łotysz, S. Personal correspondence, 31 January 2014.

29 King and Woolmans, *The assassination of the Archduke: Sarajevo 1914 and the murder that changed the world*, 284.

30 Connolly, K. 22 June 2004. 'Found: the gun that shook the world', *www.telegraph.co.uk/news/worldnews/europe/austria/1465206/Found-the-gun-that-shook-the-world.html* (accessed 12 April 2014).

31 King and Woolmans, *The assassination of the Archduke: Sarajevo 1914 and the murder that changed the world*, 284.

32 Anon. 2002. Primary Documents: Archduke Franz Ferdinand's assassination, 28 June 1914, www.uintahbasintah.org/usdocuments/doc40.pdf (accessed 23 October 2016).

33 The Internet Pathology Laboratory for Medical Education. n.d. 'Firearms Tutorial', http://library.med.utah.edu/WebPath/TUTORIAL/GUNS/GUNBLST.html (accessed 5 November 2016). This is however the colloquial definition. What it actually means is the range within which a projectile travels on a flat trajectory (i.e. much further than the modern 'point blank' would suggest).

34 May, A. J. 1966. *The passing of the Hapsburg monarchy, 1914–1918*, Vol. 1, Philadelphia, 37.

35 Otner, M. C. Personal correspondence, 22 August 2013.

36 *New York Times*. 'Heir to Austria's throne is slain with his wife by a Bosnian youth to avenge seizure of his country', 1.

37 HSH Princess Sophie von Hohenberg, Personal correspondence, 17 January 2014.

PRELIMINARY TESTING

1 Traynor, 'The Archduke and the bullet-proof vest', 153–5, on which much of this chapter is based.

2 Collins, 'The bullet-proof priest', 54–5.

3 Traynor, 'The Archduke and the bullet-proof vest', 153.

4 Washington, DC, Library of Congress, Manuscript Division, Series 14, reel 453, 151, 'Theodore Roosevelt Papers', n.d.

5 Washington, DC, Library of Congress, Manuscript Division, Series 14, reel 453, 152, 'Theodore Roosevelt Papers', n.d.

6 Zeglen, C. 'Bullet-proof fabric Patent No. 577,999', National Archives at Kansas City, Record Group: 241 Creator: Department of Commerce, Patent and Trademark Office Series: Patent Case Files, 1836–1993 National Archives Identifier: 302050.

7 Zeglen, C. 'Bullet-proof fabric Patent No. 577,999'.

8 Zeglen, C. 'Bullet-proof fabric Patent No. 577,999'.

9 Zeglen, C. 'Bullet-proof fabric Patent No. 577,999'.

10 Powder was purchased from Henry Krank & Company Ltd, Pudsey, UK.

11 This figure is an average of six rounds chronographed before the test shot was taken.

12 Established at twelve inches in ten per cent ballistic gelatine, on the basis that a bullet might have to pass through the human body at a variety of different angles and therefore depths. See

Patrick, U. W. 1989. 'Handgun wounding factors and effectiveness', http://gundata.org/images/fbi-handgun-ballistics.pdf (accessed 12 December 2016).

13 Washington, DC, Library of Congress, Manuscript Division, Series 14, reel 453, 156, 'Theodore Roosevelt Papers', n.d.

THE ZEGLEN BULLET-PROOF CLOTH CO. CATALOGUE

1 Washington, DC, Library of Congress, Manuscript Division, Series 14, reel 453, 148, 'Theodore Roosevelt Papers', n.d.

2 Washington, DC, Library of Congress, Manuscript Division, Series 14, reel 453, 150, 'Theodore Roosevelt Papers', n.d.

3 Washington, DC, Library of Congress, Manuscript Division, Series 14, reel 453, 150, 'Theodore Roosevelt Papers', n.d.

4 Washington, DC, Library of Congress, Manuscript Division, Series 14, reel 453, 151, 'Theodore Roosevelt Papers', n.d.

5 Łotysz, 'Tailored to the times', 172.

6 *Annual Reports of the War Department for the Fiscal Year Ended June 30, 1898*. Report of the Chief of Ordnance, Washington, 1899, 91. For a description of the purpose of the Springfield Armory see Łotysz, 'Tailored to the times', n. 59.

7 Łotysz, 'Tailored to the times', 173.

8 Anon. 1897. 'Bullet proof hunting coats', *Forest and Stream: A Journal of Outdoor Life, Travel, Nature Study, Shooting, Fishing, Yachting*, 49.19, 1.

9 Washington, DC, Library of Congress, Manuscript Division, Series 14, reel 453, 154, 'Theodore Roosevelt Papers', n.d.

10 Łotysz, 'Tailored to the times', 173.

11 *Morning Oregonian*. 5 November 1897. '*Not safe at 300 yards*', 9; cited in Łotysz, 'Tailored to the times: the story of Casimir Zeglen's silk bullet-proof vest', 173, n. 61.

12 Łotysz, 'Tailored to the times', 173. It is Łotysz's belief that Zeglen's 'disappointment and bitterness would not have been diminished by the fact that the experiment was not carried out properly'.

13 Washington, DC, Library of Congress, Manuscript Division, Series 14, reel 453, 154, 'Theodore Roosevelt Papers', n.d.

14 Anon. n.d. 'The Krag Rifle', www.frfrogspad.com/kragrifl.htm#Ammunition (accessed 12 December 2016).

15 Ferguson, Personal correspondence, 12 December 2016.

16 Łotysz, 'Tailored to the times', 176.

17 *Washington Post*, 20 June 1897. '*Willing to be Target*', 20.

18 Łotysz, 'Tailored to the times', 173.

19 Voyennoye ministerstvo. Glavnoye artilleriyskoye upravleniye (Ministry of War. Main Artillery Administration), 28 March 1905, file 38816, ACR. See Łotysz, 'Tailored to the times', n. 86.

20 Zeglen, C. 29 May 1905. Letter to P. Smolikowski, file 38814, ACR. In Łotysz, 'Tailored to the times', note 87–9.

21 Łotysz, 'Tailored to the times', 177.

22 Dean, *Helmets and body armor in modern warfare,* 162–3.

23 Dean, *Helmets and body armor in modern warfare,* 150.

AIM FOR THE HEAD

1 Translated from Polish by S. Łotysz from 'Od Redakcji', 174–5.

2 Bosdan, J. 21 March 1915. 'Claim Ferdinand victim of Austro-German plot', *Boston Daily Globe*, 9, and Łotysz, 'Tailored to the times', 164.

3 'Od Redakcji', 174–75.

4 Traynor, 'The Archduke and the bullet-proof vest', 152.

5 HSH Princess Sophie von Hohenberg, Personal correspondence, 17 January 2014.

6 It was reported that 'The Kaiser was terribly shocked', and that King Edward and his family 'were poignant with grief.' In addition the Pope 'was greatly distressed.' See *The Timaru Herald*, 4 February 1908. '*The Portuguese assassinations*', 5.

7 *The Timaru Herald*, 'The Portuguese assassinations', 5.

8 De Meneses, F. R. (2010) *Afonso Costa: Portugal – the peace conferences of 1919–23 and their aftermath*, London: Haus, 3.

9 *The Timaru Herald*, 'The Portuguese assassinations', 5.

10 Łotysz, Personal communication.

11 Washington, DC, Library of Congress, Manuscript Division, Series 14, reel 453, 150, 'Theodore Roosevelt Papers', n.d.

12 US Department of Justice (2001), *Selection and application guide to personal body armor: NIJ guide 100–01*, Rockville, MD, National Institute of Justice, 15.

13 Traynor, 'The Archduke and the bullet-proof vest', 158.

14 Botha, A., Personal correspondence, 2 April 2014. The measurement of the 'back side signature' is the energy delivered to tissue by a non-penetrating projectile.

15 Edwards, T. Personal correspondence, 2 January 2014.

16 Edwards, Personal correspondence, 2 January 2014.

17 Edwards, Personal correspondence, 2 January 2014.

18 Łotysz, 'Tailored to the times', 177. 'The mistrust of patent law was quite symptomatic for immigrants from Polish Galicia, a province with a much lower industrial culture.' See also Łotysz, S. 2013. 'Wynalazczość polska w Stanach Zjednoczonych', Warszawa, Aspra-JR, 258–9.

19 *Washington Post*, 'Bullet-proof priest', 25.

20 *Quincy Weekly Whig*, 'New bullet-proof cloth invented by a priest in Chicago', 2.

21 Łotysz, 'Tailored to the times', 167; *Washington Post*, 'Bullet-proof priest', 25.

22 The centiNewton per tex (cN/tex) is an unit officially adopted by the International System of Units and used worldwide except for the USA and UK, where gram per denier (g/d) is most commonly used unit. The conversion rate is: 1 cN/tex equals 0.1132 g/d. See, Łotysz, 'Tailored to the times', n. 27.

23 Ghosh, P. 2004. *Fibre science and technology*, New Delhi, 100 and 81. In other words, 'the strength of silk thread is similar to the one of steel of equal weight. Silk is also five times weaker than Kevlar®, modern aramid fibre commonly used in the manufacture of bulletproof vests. Breaking tenacity of Kevlar® fibre is approximately 194 cN/tex.' In Łotysz, 'Tailored to the times', n. 28. See also: Goswami, B. C., Anandjiwala, R. D. and Hall, D. M. 2004. *Textile sizing*, New York, 73–4.

24 Lee, Y. W. 1999. 'Silk reeling and testing manual', *FAO Agricultural Services Bulletin*, 136, 11. However flax fibre has 'slightly greater tensile strength than silk.' See also Łotysz, 'Tailored to the times', n. 29.

PURE SILK

1 Zeglen, C. 'Bullet-proof fabric Patent No. 604,870', National Archives at Kansas City, Record Group: 241 Creator: Department of Commerce, Patent and Trademark Office Series: Patent Case Files, 1836–1993 National Archives Identifier: 302050.

2 Zeglen, 'Bullet-proof fabric Patent No. 604,870'.

3 Zeglen, 'Bullet-proof fabric Patent No. 604,870'.

4 Zeglen, 'Bullet-proof fabric Patent No. 604,870'.

5 Zeglen, 'Bullet-proof fabric Patent No. 604,870'.

FRANZ FERDINAND'S VEST?

1 This was 2 lbs (1 kg) more than my estimated weight for the armour.

CONCLUSION

1 'Shooting "bullet-proof" vest full of holes in test', *Chicago Record-Herald*, 9 May 1913; Łotysz, 'Tailored to the times', 178.

2 Łotysz, 'Tailored to the times', 178.

3 See Abbott, P. 2017. *Sir Arthur Conan Doyle and the campaign for body armour, 1914–1918*, Leeds.

4 US patent no. 876,616 (14 January 1908) and US patent no. 977,357 (29 November 1910). These patents were cited in later inventions submitted by inventors representing companies such as Daimler-Benz, Michelin and Bridgestone. Zeglen advertised his tyres as bulletproof and resistant to punctures. Most importantly, however, they withstood the mileage three times greater than typical cotton-cord tyres: see The American Rubber and Fabric Company,1911, *Zeglen puncture and blow-out proof tires*, Philadelphia; cited in Łotysz, 'Tailored to the times', 186 n. 113.

BIBLIOGRAPHY

PRIMARY SOURCES: ARCHIVES

Italy

Archivio della Congregazione della Risurrezione, Rome

Voyennoye ministerstvo. 28 March 1905. 'Glavnoye artilleriyskoye upravleniye' [Ministry of War. Main Artillery Administration], file 38816.

Zeglen, C. 29 May 1905. 'Letter to P. Smolikowski', file 38814.

USA

Library of Congress, Washington

Theodore Roosevelt Papers, Index. Vol. 3 R-Z. Manuscript Division, Library of Congress.

Theodore Roosevelt Papers, Series 14 reel 453. Manuscript Division, Library of Congress.

National Archives at Kansas City

Zeglen. C., 'Patent of Casimir Zeglen, for bullet-proof fabric, March 1897'. *Patent number 577,999.*

Zeglen. C., 'Patent of Casimir Zeglen, for bullet-proof fabric, March 1897'. *Patent number 578,000.*

Zeglen. C., 'Patent of Casimir Zeglen, for bullet-proof fabric, May 1898'. *Patent number 604,870.*

UK

British Patent Office

Zeglen. C., 'Improvements in Bullet-proof fabrics, April 1897, Zeglen's complete specification'. *British Patent No. 5536*, 2 March 1897. Accepted 3 April 1897.

PRIMARY SOURCES: NEWSPAPERS

Boston Daily Globe
Chicago Daily Tribune
The Daily Republican
Los Angeles Times
Morning Oregonian
New York Times
Quincy Daily Journal
The Quincy Weekly Wig

The Saint Paul Globe
The Telegraph
Timaru Herald
Washington Post

SECONDARY SOURCES

Abbott, P. 2017, Sir Arthur Conan Doyle and the campaign for body armour, 1914–1918, Leeds.

Allsop, K. 1990. *The bootleggers and their era,* Chicago.

Anastasakis, O., Madden, D. and Roberts, E. (eds.) 2016. *Balkan legacies of the Great War: the past is never dead,* London.

Anderson, F. M. and Hershey, A. S. 1918. 'Handbook for the diplomatic history of Europe, Asia, and Africa, 1870–1914', https://archive.org/stream/handbookfordiplo00ande/handbookfordiplo00ande_djvu.txt (accessed 27 November 2016).

Anon. 1897. 'Bullet proof hunting coats', *Forest and stream: a journal of outdoor life, travel, nature study, shooting, fishing, yachting,* 49.19, 1.

Anon. 1927. 'Od Redakcji', *Naokoło Świata,* 41, 174–175.

Anon. n.d. 'The Krag Rifle', www.frfrogspad.com/kragrifl.htm#Ammunition (accessed 12 December 2016).

Barclay, D. E. 1992. 'Ritual, ceremonial, and the "invention" of a monarchical tradition in nineteenth-century Prussia', in Duchhardt, H., Jackson, R. A. and Sturdy, D. (eds.), *European monarchy: its evolution and practice from Roman Antiquity to modern times,* Stuttgart, 207–220.

Barrell, J. 2000. *Imagining the king's death: figurative treason, fantasies of regicide, 1793–1796,* Oxford.

Beatty, J. 2012. *The lost history of 1914,* London.

The Buffalo History Museum, 'Collection highlights', www.buffalohistory.org/Explore/Collections.aspx (accessed 20 February 2018).

Busca Biografía. n.d. 'Manuel Enrique Araujo', www.buscabiografias.com/biografia/verDetalle/8304/Manuel%20Enrique%20Araujo (accessed 27 September 2016).

Cannadine, D. 1983. 'The context, performance and meaning of ritual: the British monarchy and the "invention of tradition", *c.*1820–1977', in Hobsbawm, E. J. and Ranger, T. O. (eds.), *The invention of tradition,* Cambridge, 101–64.

Canzanella. J. 2010. *Innocence and anarchy,* Bloomington.

Chaliand, G. and Blin, A. 2007. 'The "golden age" of terrorism', in Chaliand, G. and Blin, A. (eds.), *The history of terrorism from antiquity to al Qaeda,* Berkeley, CA.

Chasteen, J. 1984. 'Manuel Enrique Araujo and the failure of reform in El Salvador, 1911–1913', *South Eastern Latin Americanist* 28:2, 1–15.

Chief of Ordnance, Report of the (1899) *Annual Reports of the War Department for the Fiscal Year ended June 30, 1898.* Washington.

Chinn, G. M. 1955. *The machine gun, Volume IV: design analysis of automatic firing mechanisms and related components,* Washington.

Christmas, W. 1914. *The life of King George of Greece,* New York.

Clark, C. 2013. *The sleepwalkers: how Europe went to war in 1914,* London.

Collins, P. 2005. 'The bullet-proof priest', *New Scientist,* 2496, 54–5.

Cormack, A. J. R. 1971. *Small arms profile 2: Browning automatic pistols and the Hi-Power,* Chichester.

David, S. 2014. *100 days to victory: how the Great War was fought and won 1914–1918,* London.

Dean, B. 1920. *Helmets and body armor in modern warfare,* Yale.

Dedijer, V. 1966. *The road to Sarajevo,* New York.

Dietze, C. and Schenk, F. 2009. 'Traditionelle Herrscher in moderner Gefahr. Soldatisch-aristokratische Tugendhaftigkeit und das Konzept der Sicherheit im späten 19. Jahrhundert', *Geschichte und Gesellschaft,* 35(3), 368–401.

Dunston, S. 1984. *Flak jackets, 20th century military body armour,* London.

Friedman, J. 2017. 'What is a Velo Dog?', www.velodogs.com (accessed 20 February 2018).

Ferguson, J. 2016. '"You never dreamt of a poysoned bullet": "forbidden" ammunition from the 16th century to the present', Unpublished conference paper at Firearms and the Common Law Tradition, Aspen Institute, Washington DC.

Ferguson, J. and Traynor, L. 2014. 'Browning Modèle 1900 pistol' https://collections.royalarmouries.org/first-world-war/type/rac-narrative-73.html (accessed 19 September 2016).

Ferguson, J., and Traynor, L. 2014. 'Pistole 08 (P08) Parabellum pistol' https://collections.royalarmouries.org/first-world-war/type/rac-narrative-69.html (accessed 19 September 2016).

Ferguson, N. ed. 1997. *Virtual history: alternatives and counterfactuals*, London.

Ford, F. L. 1976. 'Assassination in the eighteenth century: the dog that did not bark in the night', *Proceedings of the American Philosophical Society*, 120(3), 211–15.

Ford, F. L. 1985. *Political murder: from tyrannicide to terrorism*, Cambridge, MA.

Geifman, A. 1993. *Thou shalt kill: revolutionary terrorism in Russia, 1894–1917*, Princeton.

Goforth, W. E. 1992. *Iver Johnson Arm & Cycle Works, Handguns 1871–1978*, Chino Valley.

Ghosh, P. 2004. *Fibre science and technology,* New Delhi.

Goswami, B. C., Anandjiwala, R. D & Hall, D. M. 2004. *Textile sizing,* New York.

Harrach, F., 'The memoir of Count Franz von Harrach', www.firstworldwar.com/source/harrachmemoir.htm (accessed 5 October 2015).

Hoffman, R. G. 2015. 'The age of assassination: monarchy and nation in nineteenth-century Europe', in Wachsmann, N. and Rüger, J. (eds.), *Rewriting German history: new perspectives on modern Germany*, London, 121–41.

Hogg, I. V. 1979. *The complete handgun 1300 to the present,* London.

Hubac-Occhipinti, O. 2007. 'Anarchist terrorists of the nineteenth century', in Chaliand, G. and Blin, A. (eds.), *The history of terrorism from antiquity to al Qaeda*, Berkeley, CA, 113–31.

imssu.org. 2006. 'The 1895 Nagant Revolver', www.imssu.org/articles/the%201895%20nagant%20revolver.pdf (accessed 31 December 2016).

The Internet Pathology Laboratory for Medical Education, 'Firearms tutorial', http://library.med.utah.edu/WebPath/TUTORIAL/GUNS/GUNBLST.html (accessed 5 November 2016).

Jensen, R. B. 2015. *The battle against anarchist terrorism: an international History, 1878–1934,* Cambridge.

Jones, S. J. 2011. *The silence (Viennese Mysteries)*, Sutton.

June, D. L. 2008. *Introduction to executive protection: Second edition,* Boca Raton.

Kekkonen, P. T. 1999. 'ARCANE, or forbidden knowledge about handloading', http://guns.connect.fi/gow/arcane2.html (accessed 27 September 2016).

King, G. and Woolmans, S. 2013. *The assassination of the Archduke: Sarajevo 1914 and the murder that changed the world*, London.

Lafore, L. 1971. *The long fuse; an interpretation of the origins of World War I,* New York.

Lee, Y. W. 1999. 'Silk reeling and testing manual', *FAO Agricultural Services Bulletin*, 136, 11.

Lincoln, W. B. 1983. *The Romanovs: autocrats of all the Russians*, New York.

Łotysz, S. 2009. 'Historia sporu o pewien wynalazek: Jan Szczepanik, Kazimierz Żegleń i kamizelka kuloodporna'. *Analecta: Studia i Materiały z Dziejów Nauki*, 18, 1–2, 349–66.

Łotysz, S. 2014. 'Tailored to the times: the story of Casimir Zeglen's silk bullet-proof vest', *Arms & Armour*, Vol. 11 No. 2, 164–86.

MacMillan, M. 2014. *The war that ended peace: how Europe abandoned peace for the First World War,* London.

Maislish, D. 2012. *Assassination: the royal family's 1000 year curse*, Brighton.

Marcovitz, H. 2013. *Pancho Villa*, Philadelphia.

Masssey, I. M. (tr and ed.) 1953. *The origins of the war of 1914 Vol 2*, Oxford.

May, A. J. 1966. *The passing of the Hapsburg monarchy, 1914–1918,* Vol. 1, Philadelphia.

McMeekin, S. 2014. *July 1914: countdown to war*, London.

Mijatović, G. 1917. *The memoirs of a Balkan diplomatist*, London.

Motley, J. L. 1883. *The rise of the Dutch Republic: a history,* New York.

Murphy, P. T. 2012. *Shooting Victoria: madness, mayhem and the rebirth of the British monarchy*, London.

Österreichische Staatsarchiv. n.d. 'Attentat auf Kaiser Franz Joseph', www.oesta.gv.at/site/cob__41967/currentpage__0/6644/ default.asp (accessed 27 September 2016).

Patrick, U. W. 1989. 'Handgun wounding factors and effectiveness', http://gundata.org/images/fbi-handgun-ballistics.pdf (accessed 12 December 2016).

Pauli, H. 1966. *The secret of Sarajevo; the story of Franz Ferdinand and Sophie* London.

Paulmann, J. 2000. *Pomp und Politik: Monarchenbegegnungen in Europa zwischen Ancien Régime und Erstem Weltkrieg*, Munich.

Pilipiuk, A. 2005. 'The forgotten genius', http://andrzej.pilipiuk.w.interiowo.pl/dane/geniusz.html (accessed 24 October 2016).

Plunkett, J. 2003. *Queen Victoria: first media monarch*, Oxford.

Polvinen, T. 1995. *Imperial borderland: Bobrikov and the attempted Russification of Finland, 1898–1904*, London.

Popenker, M. 1999–2018. 'FN Browning M1900', http://world.guns.ru/handguns/hg/be/fn-browning-m1900-e.html (accessed 20 February 2018).

Popenker, M. 1999–2018. 'Nagant m.1895', http://modernfirearms.net/handguns/double-action-revolvers/rus/nagan-arr-195-e.html (accessed 20 February 2018).

Porter, L. 2010. *Assassination: a history of political murder*, London.

Roberts, I. 2016. 'The Black Hand and the Sarajevo Conspiracy' in Anastasakis, O, Madden et al (eds.), *Balkan legacies of the Great War: the past is never dead*, London, 23–43.

Rogan, E. 2015. *The fall of the Ottomans: the Great War in the Middle East, 1914–1920*, New York.

Remak, J. 1959. *Sarajevo: the story of a political murder*, New York.

RSC Advancing Chemical Science. n.d. 'The murder of Rasputin', www.rsc.org/learn-chemistry/content/filerepository/CMP/00/001/680/The_murder_of_Rasputin.pdf?v=1353967419600 (accessed 29 December 2016).

Sacks, N. 2016. *WWI the causes*, Minneapolis.

Schoultz, D. n.d. 'What powder should you use?' www.blackpowderrifleaccuracy.com/powder.html (accessed 12 September 2015).

Sebag Montefiore, S. 2016. *The Romanovs 1613–1918*, London.

Sisi Museum. n.d. 'Assassination', www.hofburg-wien.at/en/things-to-know/sisi-museum/tour-of-the-sisi-museum/assassination.html (accessed 27 September 2016).

Smith, D. J. 2009. *One morning in Sarajevo*, London.

Smith, D. 2012. *Former people*, London.

Smith, D. 2016. *Rasputin: the biography*, London.

Stevenson, D. 2004. *Cataclysm: the First World War as political tragedy*, New York.

Strachan, H. 2001. *The First World War, Volume 1: To arms*, Oxford.

Ternon, Y. 2007. 'Russian terrorism, 1878–1908', in Chaliand, G. and Blin, A. (eds.), *The history of terrorism from antiquity to al Qaeda*, Berkeley, CA, 132–74.

Tilstone, W. J., Savage, K. A., and Clark, L. A. 2006. *Forensic science: an encyclopaedia of history, methods, and techniques*, Santa Barbara.

Traynor, L. 2014. 'The Archduke and the bullet-proof vest: 19th century innovation versus 20th century firepower', *Arms & Armour*, Vol. 11 No. 2, Autumn, 147–63.

Traynor, L. 2014. 'Browning modèle 1910 pistol', https://collections.royalarmouries.org/first-world-war/type/rac-narrative-74.html (accessed 20 September 2016).

Traynor, L. 2014. 'Colt model of 1911 pistol', https://collections.royalarmouries.org/first-world-war/type/rac-narrative-75.html (accessed 20 September 2016).

Traynor, L. 2014. 'Nagant model 1895 revolver', https://collections.royalarmouries.org/first-world-war/type/rac-narrative-78.html (accessed 20 September 2016).

Trumball, W. & Inglehart, W. M. 1893. 'The world's Columbian Exposition, Chicago, 1893 / a full description of the buildings and exhibits in all departments', https://archive.org/stream/worldscolumbiane00whit/worldscolumbiane00whit_djvu.txt (accessed 12 December 2016).

Turner, L. C. F. 1970. *Origins of the First World War*, London.

Vanderlinden, A. 2001. *The Belgian Browning pistols 1889–1949*, Greensboro.

Vanderlinden, A. 2013. *FN Browning pistols: side arms that shaped world history*, Greensboro.

Vulich, N. L. 2013. *Killing the presidents: presidential assassinations and assassination attempts*, USA.

Warlow, T. A. 1996. *Firearms, the law and forensic ballistics*, London.

Zhuk, A. B. 1995. *The illustrated encyclopaedia of handguns*, London.